The
Divine-Human
Family

Adventist Pioneer Library

A Service of
Light Bearers Ministry
37457 Jasper Lowell Rd
Jasper, OR, 97438, USA
(877) 585-1111
www.LightBearers.org

Originally published in the 1895 General Conference Bulletin.

Published in the USA

ISBN: 978-1-61455-025-9

The
Divine-Human
Family

For this cause I bow my knees unto the Father of our
Lord Jesus Christ, of whom the whole family
in heaven and earth is named. Ephesians 3:14-15.

1895 General Conference Series

Fred Bischoff, Compiler

By
W. W. Prescott

W. W. PRESCOTT (1855-1944)

CONTENTS

PREFACE

The historical setting of these studies by W. W. Prescott, from the 1895 General Conference Session held in Battle Creek, Michigan, is very helpful and important. Prescott had just recently left his position as president of Battle Creek College that he had held since 1885, to focus more on his duties as General Conference Education Director, which he had been since 1887. Prescott's work in the educational ministry, and church administration, would continue for many years.

The most important influence in 1895 was that of the General Conference Session held seven years earlier in Minneapolis, Minnesota, and the issues surrounding it, in regard to what God was longing to give to those carrying the three angels' messages to the world. This "new" light was to impact every believer, their home lives, the ministries of the church in which they worked, and all of their witness to the world. The following extracts from a biographical review of Prescott address some of these details.

MESSAGE OF MINNEAPOLIS

The influence of the Minneapolis Conference in 1888 reached the college. Ellen White worked diligently that the message the Lord had given at Minneapolis would be heard at Battle Creek. Some six weeks after the conference session, the week of Prayer planned for the church in Battle Creek December 15-22 ended up lasting one month. Ellen White described that in these "revival services... the principle topic dwelt upon was justification by faith." (RH2/12/1889, in 3Bio420).

On Thursday, December 20, Ellen White wrote in her diary, "I spoke to the college students. The Lord gave me the word which seemed to reach hearts. Professor Prescott arose and attempted to speak, but his heart was too full. There he stood five minutes in complete silence, weeping. When he did speak he said, 'I am glad I am a Christian.' He made very pointed remarks. His heart seemed to be broken by the Spirit of the Lord...." (Ms25, 1888, in 3Bio421). Prescott's response to the Spirit's moving is heart warming.

Speaking further of the Scriptural light the Lord had given through brothers Jones and Waggoner, Ellen White wrote on March 10, 1890, "I am much pleased to learn that Professor Prescott is giving the same lessons in his class to the students that Brother Waggoner has been giving. He is presenting the covenants." (Letter 30, 1890, in *1888 Materials*, p. 623).

Later that year, Ellen White described the "wonderful" December 27 Sabbath meeting. "Nearly the whole congregation presented themselves for prayers, and among them, Brethren Prescott and Smith. The *Extra* in the *Review and Herald* [Dec. 23, 1890] was read, and the testimony of all was that the power of God attended the reading of the article. They said that this made a deep impression.... Professor Prescott made a confession dating back to Minneapolis, and this made a deep impression. He wept much. Elder Smith said that testimony meant him; said that he felt that it was addressed to him, but he stopped there and went no further. But both placed themselves as there repentant, seeking the Lord. Well, they said they had never had such a meeting in Battle Creek, and yet the work must be carried on, for it was just begun...." (Lt 32, 1891, in *1888 Materials*, pp. 850, 851)

The message continued to do its work against stiff opposition. Both A. T. Jones and E. J. Waggoner were finally allowed to lecture at Battle Creek College. Prescott, gradually seeing more and more light in the Christ-centered message, worked hard as a peace-maker and consensus builder between the opposing parties. After Ellen White was exiled to Australia in 1891, her writings on the message kept the Spirit's appeal before the church. In the November 22, 1892 *Review and Herald*, she wrote, "The time of test is just upon us, for the loud cry of the third angel has already begun in the revelation of the righteousness of Christ, the sin-pardoning Redeemer. This is the beginning of the light of the angel whose glory shall fill the whole earth. For it is the work of every one to whom the message of warning has come, to lift up Jesus, to present him to the world as revealed in types, as shadowed in symbols, as manifested in the revelations of the prophets, as unveiled in the lessons given to his disciples and in the wonderful miracles wrought for the sons of men." (*1888 Material*, p. 1073).

The effect of this article on the college, along with other timely testimonies from Ellen White, led to a vigorous revival. The rest of the school term was disrupted by long chapels, seasons of prayer and confession, and times of testimonies. Prescott, in reading a letter from Ellen White to the students, was moved to tears, and confessed again his previous resistance to the message. Sadly, Uriah Smith viewed the events as "excitement." Thus the spiritual consensus the church greatly needed was never experienced (Fred Bischoff, "W. W. Prescott, Messenger of God's Invitation, 'Come, for all things are now ready...'", *Lest We Forget*, Vol. 10, No. 1, pp. 3, 4).

MINISTERIAL INSTITUTES

Against a background of minimal training for our ministers, and the controversy that boiled over at Minneapolis, Prescott designed a five-month ministerial institute for ministers. The first began in October of 1889, with 157 attendees. Prescott, Uriah Smith, and E. J. Waggoner were instructors.

In spite of Ellen White's strong endorsement, Waggoner's views were actively opposed by Smith, and led to her personally joining some of the early morning dialogues. Her letters, manuscripts, and diary entries written during the institute provide essential insights into what God was attempting to accomplish in these settings to prepare a people for Christ's coming. [The reader is encouraged to read the chronological collection of her writings on these issues in *The Ellen G. White 1888 Materials*.]

These institutes continued until 1896, by which time the colleges had developed more complete ministerial training courses. However, Ellen White lamented to the GC President in November of 1892 that ministers were not being benefited as they ought to have been by these gatherings. She said they either haggled over the truth, or having assented to it, kept it in "the outer court," not letting it permeate their lives in the "little things," particularly in the home setting (PH002:25, 26). She again spoke to the delegates at the GC Session in 1901 of the assent to this truth with no change in life or ministry. This counterfeit "faith" actually masked a deep-seated rebellion, which later that year she said might cause God's people to remain in this world "many more years." (*1888 Materials*, p. 1743; SpM202) (*Ibid.*, p. 5).

IMPACT ON EDUCATION

Prescott developed a master list of Adventist teachers (church employed or not) and began a program of teachers' training institutes. Two significant conventions were held, one in 1891 at Harbor Springs, Michigan, and one in 1894 at another location. Both focused on making SDA education more Bible centered. At the 1891 gathering a four-year curriculum was first developed for ministerial training. At the 1894 meeting, Prescott and A. T. Jones produced a four-year syllabus of Bible teaching for non-ministerial students. Plans were even laid for a graduate program (which was not realized for another sixty years) and an education journal (which took three years to begin).

At the January 1893 GC Session Prescott reported that the Harbor Springs meeting "marked a remarkable change in the history of our educational work. Our minds were impressed there as never before with the idea that the purpose of educational work was to teach us of God in his revealed word and his works, and in his dealings with men, that all education should be planned upon such a basis and carried out in such a way that the result would be a more intimate knowledge of God, not merely as a theory but as an experience."

He further observed, "...The Bible should be studied as the gospel of Christ from first to last; and in which it should be made to appear that all the doctrines held by Seventh-day Adventists were simply the gospel of Christ rightly understood, and that the basis was the proper understanding of the whole Scriptures, and not merely a limited study of a few portions of the Scriptures.... It has not been the purpose to put in the back-ground those doctrines which distinguish us, but to make it appear that these are simply the doctrines of the Bible as a whole; that the third angel's message is simply the gospel, and that the message properly understood is an understanding of all the Scriptures, and that all of our doctrines have their basis in a proper knowledge of the gospel, and grown out of a belief in Jesus Christ as a living personal Saviour." (*GC Bulletin*, 1893, p. 350) (*Ibid.*, pp. 5, 6).

GENERAL CONFERENCE SESSIONS

Prescott's presentations at the General Conference Sessions after Minneapolis, leading into the 1895 Session from which "The Divine-

Human Family" series is taken, provide a view of what themes he addressed. As with the series we reproduce here, the other talks are available from the CD-ROM collection.

1891 GC Session
> The Calling and Work of the Ministry

1893 GC Session
> The Promise of the Holy Spirit, No. 1, 2, 3, 4, 5
>
> Sabbath

1895 GC Session
> The Divine-Human Family, No. 1, 2, 3, 4, 5, 6
>
> Education
>
> The Word of God, No. 1, 2, 3, 4, 5, 6, 7, 8, 9, 10
>
> Christ and the Holy Spirit

One should be able to see from the studies on "The Divine-Human Family" as well as the Armadale Camp Meeting Series (from later in 1895, after his arrival in Australia; these have been republished separately), that Prescott was open to the "most precious" truth that the Spirit was revealing to those proclaiming the soon coming of Jesus. The corporate, universal themes were rightfully placed as a foundation underneath the individual themes that should flow out of the gospel, and complete the whole of God's purpose in the salvation of souls. It must become clear to us, that if we limit the recall of the foundation truths, the personal experience intended will also be limited. One can stand tall only to the proportion as he grasps how deeply his roots are anchored in Jesus Christ.

This seems clearly to be the intent of the following statement, made after the 1895 Session, and before the Armadale Camp Meeting, just after Prescott arrived in Australia.

> Those who, since the Minneapolis meeting, have had the privilege of listening to the words spoken by the messengers of God, Elder A.T. Jones, Prof. Prescott, Brn. E. J. Waggoner, O. A. Olsen, and many others, at the campmeetings and ministerial institutes, have had the

invitation, "Come, for all things are now ready. Come to the supper prepared for you." Light, heaven's light, has been shining. The trumpet has given a certain sound. Those who have made their various excuses for neglecting to respond to the call, have lost much. The light has been shining upon justification by faith and the imputed righteousness of Christ. Those who receive and act in the light given, will, in their teachings, give evidence that the message of Christ crucified, a risen Saviour ascended into the heavens to be our advocate, is the wisdom and power of God in the conversion of souls, bringing them back to their loyalty to Christ. These are our themes,--Christ crucified for our sins, Christ risen from the dead, Christ our intercessor before God; and closely connected with these is the office-work of the Holy Spirit, the representative of Christ, sent forth with divine power and gifts for men (*1888 Materials*, p. 1455.2; *Letter* 86, 1895, September 25, 1895 to Edson White).

NOTES

BIBLE REFERENCES

Bible references are given with the full name of the book.

ELLEN WHITE'S WRITINGS REFERENCES

Quotes from Ellen White's writings are supplied with current references in brackets.

GENERAL CONFERENCE BULLETIN REFERENCES AND SETTINGS

Reference to Sermon No. 1

ACCORDING to appointment, the first meeting of the Institute was held in the Tabernacle at 10 A. M., Friday, February 1. There were about 300 present, and the first hour was occupied by Elder O. A. Olsen in an address, an abstract of which appears elsewhere. At 11:15 Dr. Kellogg opened a series of lectures on topics kindred to the work and design of the Medical Missionary and Benevolent Association. In the afternoon the first meeting of the Council was held, and was addressed by Elder Olsen. In the evening Prof. W. W. Prescott took up during the first hour the subject of the Divine-Human Family, treating particularly of the Head of the Family. This was followed by a discourse by Elder A. T. Jones on the Third Angel's Message. {February 4, 1895 N/A, GCB 1.1}

These addresses are given quite fully in another place and need not be particularly alluded to here. There was a goodly attendance from abroad, and in the evening the Tabernacle was well filled. There was felt by all the prevailing influence of the Spirit of God. It is evident that the servants of God have come to the meetings with a sense of the solemnity of the times upon them, expecting to receive light and power from above. If this be so, and they unitedly seek for it, they will obtain the rich blessing they desire, for God is waiting to bestow heaven's richest blessings upon us. The first day's meetings lead us to believe that the occasion will be one of great power and blessing to the waiting people of God. {February 4, 1895 N/A, GCB 1.2} [No. 1 began at 8.1]

Setting for Sermon No. 2

SUNDAY, FEBRUARY 3 [heading shown here:] {February 6, 1895 N/A, GCB 19.3} [No. 2 began at 24.5]

Setting for Sermon No. 3

MONDAY, FEBRUARY 4 [heading shown here:] {February 6, 1895 N/A, GCB 35.1} [No. 3 began at 41.7]

Setting for Sermon No. 4

FRIDAY, FEBRUARY 8 [heading shown here:] {February 11, 1895 N/A, GCB 101.5} [No. 4 begins at 107.7]

Setting for Sermon No. 5

(NOTE: mistakenly labeled in the *GC Bulletin* as No. 4 again)--

THE DIVINE-HUMAN FAMILY - NO. 4

W. W. PRESCOTT

MONDAY, FEBRUARY 11.

MEMBERSHIP MEANS SEPARATION

[begins at:] {February 15, 1895 N/A, GCB 158.1}

Setting for Sermon No. 6

(NOTE: mistakenly labeled in the *GC Bulletin* as No. 5)--

WEDNESDAY FEBRUARY 13 [heading shown here:] {February 17, 1895 N/A, GCB 178.1} [No. 6 begins at 186.3]

Sermon 1

The Head of the Family

THE one object in all our Bible study should be, not to establish theories, but to feed upon the living word. And it seems especially desirable to call attention to this principle when a large number of us who are accustomed to teaching the word come together to make a special study of it. Hence the principle should not be to learn some theory which we can tell to others, but to obtain a life which may be lived before others; and this will be the purpose in our study of the word, — simply to feed upon the word which is Spirit and which is life. And this will be the case, no matter what special phase of truth we may study. Our whole purpose will be to break the bread of life so that we may together feed upon it.

The subject which we will consider together, for a time at least, during this Institute may perhaps be designated as the Divine-Human Family. In Ephesians 3:14, 15 we read: "For this cause I bow my knees unto the Father of our Lord Jesus Christ, of whom the whole family in heaven and earth is named." The whole family in heaven and earth. And it will be our purpose to consider this idea of the family, but from this special standpoint, the Divine-Human family; and our topic for this hour will be to consider the Head of the family.

I would like to call attention, first, to the fact that the human family, considered as a human family, has one common Father. Acts 17:24-26. "God that made the world and all things therein, seeing that he is Lord of heaven and earth, dwelleth not in temples made with hands; neither is worshiped with men's hands, as though he needed anything, seeing he giveth to all life, and breath, and all things; and hath made of one blood all nations of men." This is our authorized version; the revised version leaves out the word "blood." "And he made of *one* every nation of men for to dwell on all the face of the earth." Hath made of *one* all nations of the earth; that is, Adam was the father of the human family as a human family; and when God created Adam he created the whole human family. He created all nations that are upon the earth when he created Adam. That is, in creating Adam and conferring upon him the power to beget in his own image, he saw, as it were, a fountain of life in him; and when he created Adam, he saw in Adam every human being that has been or will be upon the face of the earth, and he created every human being upon the face of the earth in Adam.

You will see how this thought is suggested in the 25th chapter of Genesis, where the birth of Jacob and Esau is recorded. Verses 19 to 23 give the record. But I call special attention to the 23rd verse. When Rebecca inquired of the Lord, he answered her, "Two nations are in thy womb." Two nations, — Jacob and Esau. In Jacob, God saw all the descendants of Jacob; in Esau, God saw all the descendants of Esau; and so, as he viewed it, there were two nations struggling together.

The same thought is further emphasized in Hebrews 7:9, 10: "And as I may say so, Levi also, who received tithes, payed tithes in Abraham. For he was yet in the loins of his father when Melchisedec met him."

These scriptures are sufficient to bring out the principle, that in Adam were all the descendants of Adam, as he was the common father of the human family. but Adam the first failed in his work, and so there came Adam the second. 1 Corinthians 15:45 and onward: "And so it is written, The first man Adam was made a living soul; the last Adam was made a quickening spirit. Howbeit that was not first which is spiritual, but that which is natural; and afterward that which is spiritual. The first man is of the earth, earthy; the second man is the Lord from heaven." And this second man, the Lord from heaven, sustains the same relation to his family that Adam sustained to *his* family. That is, he became the second father of the family.

In Colossians 3:9, 10: "Lie not one to another, seeing that ye have put off the old man with his deeds; and have put on the new man, which is renewed in knowledge after the image of him that created him." Ephesians 4:22-24: "That ye put off concerning the former conversation the old man, which is corrupt according to the deceitful lusts, and be renewed in the spirit of your mind; and that ye put on the new man which after God is created in righteousness and true holiness." Dr. Young's translation of this same text gives a little different wording, which is important. Instead of reading, "Which after God is created in righteousness," he translates more literally, "Which according to God *was* created in righteousness."

Now with these scriptures before us, we can see readily the teaching. Adam was the first man, and by yielding to sin, he received sin into human flesh, and his flesh became sinful flesh. Christ was the second man, the second father of the human family. He did no sin, neither was guile found in his mouth. After humanity in Adam had admitted sin into the flesh, that became the old man, and the old man is humanity with sin working in it. That is to say, the old man is humanity under the control of the devil, and those who are in that condition are spoken of by the Saviour in John 8 as being of their father the devil. 42nd verse and onward: "Jesus said unto them, If God were your Father, ye would love me, for I proceeded forth and came from God; neither came I of myself, but he sent me. Why do ye not understand my speech? even because ye cannot hear my word. Ye are of your father the devil, and the lusts of your father ye will do."

The old man is humanity with sin working in it; the old man is humanity under the control and direction of the devil. The new man is humanity with divinity in it, and above all and first of all, the new man is Christ Jesus, "which according to God was created in righteousness and true holiness." So we are instructed to put on the new man. Romans 13:14.

"Put ye on the Lord Jesus Christ," the new man, "and make no provision for the flesh, to fulfill the lusts thereof."

Now how did Jesus Christ become the second father of the human family? and what does it mean to us that he did become the second father of the human family? This is told in Hebrews 2:14: "Forasmuch then as the children" [he is the father] are partakers of flesh and blood, he also himself likewise took part of the same; that through death he might destroy him that had the power of death, that is, the devil; and deliver them who through fear of death were all their lifetime subject to bondage." Notice carefully; it is because the children were partakers of flesh and blood that he also himself likewise took part of the same flesh and blood. Why? In order that he might destroy him that had the power of death, that is, the devil.

This thought is suggested in 1st John 3:5." And ye know that he was manifested to take away our sins." Notice what it says. "Ye know that he *was manifested*." He WAS MANIFESTED to take away our sins. How was he manifested? He was manifested in the flesh; by becoming partaker of flesh and blood he was manifested. John says in the first chapter and second verse, "For the life was manifested, and we have seen it, and bear witness, and show unto you that eternal life, which was with the Father, and was manifested unto us." And he was manifested to take away our sins; and he was manifested by taking part in flesh and blood, that he might be seen, capable of being looked upon. but he was manifested to take away our sins. For it was necessary, in order to take away our sins, that divinity should suffer. But how could divinity suffer simply and solely as divinity for the sins of humanity? So divinity was clothed with humanity, was manifested in humanity, that there might be a human side to divinity for the suffering; that it might be possible for divinity to present a human side for the suffering; that there might be, as it were, a vulnerable side to divinity, that divinity might receive the wound: because prophecy said that his heel should be bruised, and that must be in humanity. There must be a human side to divinity in order that divinity might suffer in humanity. But divinity must suffer to take away our sins, so divinity was manifested, put into humanity, clothed with a body; clothed with flesh, with our flesh, in order that divinity might present a side capable of receiving the wound; so, "The Word was made flesh and dwelt among us," and he partook of the same flesh and blood in order "that through death he might destroy him that had the power of death, that is, the devil, and might deliver them who through fear of death [and death comes only through sin] were all their lifetime subject to bondage."

How did he take upon him that nature, that flesh and blood? he did it by birth, by being born of a woman, and the agency through which he was born of a woman was the Holy Spirit. Luke 1:35: "And the angel answered and said unto her, the Holy Ghost shall come upon thee, and the power of the highest shall overshadow thee; therefore also that holy thing which shall be born of thee shall be called the Son of God." But he was also the

Son of Man, and the head, the second head of the human family was a man, the new man, the divine-human man, the man Christ Jesus.

Now what does it mean to us that Jesus Christ became the second head of this human family? It means this: Just as, when Adam was created, all the members of the human family were created in him, so also when the second man was created "according to God in righteousness and true holiness," all the members of that family were created in him. It means that, as God saw in Adam all the members of the human family, so he saw in Christ, the second father of the family, all the members of the divine human family; so he saw in him all his sons, all his daughters, all his descendants; all that belong to the family. No matter whether they were born into the family or not. Before Jacob and Esau were born, God saw two nations there. No matter whether born into the divine-human family or not, yet God created in Christ Jesus, the new man, all the members of the divine-human family that should afterward be born into that family.

Now the fact that Christ took our flesh, and that the Word was made flesh and dwelt among us, means a great deal more than that there was a good man who lived then, and set us a good example. He was the second father, he was the representative of humanity; and it was when Jesus Christ took our human nature and was born of a woman, that humanity and divinity were joined. It was then that Jesus Christ gave himself, not simply *for* the human family but *to* the human family. That is to say, Jesus Christ joined himself *to* humanity and gave himself *to* humanity, and identified himself with humanity and became humanity; and he became we, and we were there in him. It means that Jesus Christ in himself joined humanity and divinity to all eternity to take our human nature and retain it to all eternity, and is to-day our representative in heaven, still bearing our human nature, and there is a divine-human man in heaven to-day, — Jesus Christ.

Read it in Hebrews 10:11, 12: "And every priest standeth daily ministering and offering oftentimes the same sacrifices, which can never take away sins; but this *man* after he had offered one sacrifice for sins forever sat down on the right hand of God." There is a man sitting on the right hand of God, and we sit there in him. That is what this scripture in the seventh of Hebrews, to which we have referred, has illustrated, how it is that God saw in Adam all the human family, and how that when he created Adam he created all the human family. This Scripture means a great deal more than that. Read again Hebrews 7:9, 10: "And as I may so say, Levi also, who receiveth tithes, paid tithes in Abraham. For he was yet in the loins of his father when Melchisedec met him." When Abraham paid tithes to Melchisedec, Levi paid tithes in him, for he was in the loins of his father when Melchisedec met him. All that Abraham did, Levi did in him.

Read further in the 15th chapter of 1 Corinthians, verses 21 and 22: "For since by man came death, by man came also the resurrection of the dead." You may stop a moment to think that they both came by a tree; death came by a tree, life came by a tree. Adam ate of the forbidden fruit of the tree, so death came upon the human family. Christ bore all our sins upon a tree, and by that means brought life to the human family. "By man came death; by man came also the resurrection of the dead, for as in Adam all die, even so in Christ shall all be made alive." Adam is the man through whom death came; Christ is the man through whom comes the resurrection from the dead.

Read also Romans 5:12 and onward. As we read this scripture, bear these principles in mind, and this parallel between the first Adam and the second Adam, and what we gained through the first Adam and what we gained through the second Adam. From the first Adam, sin, transitory life, death; from the second Adam, righteousness, life, — eternal life. "Wherefore, as by *one man* sin entered into the world, and death by sin; and so death passed upon all men, for that all have sinned." Revised Version, "for that all sinned." Just one act in a point of time wholly past. For that all sinned; for all did sin.

"For until the law sin was in the world: but sin is not imputed where there is no law. Nevertheless death reigned from Adam to Moses, even over them that had not sinned after the similitude of Adam's transgression, who is the figure (or type) of him that was to come. But not as the offense, so also is the free gift; for if through the offense of *one* many be dead (Revised Version, many died) much more the grace of God, and the gift by grace, which is by *one man*, Jesus Christ, hath abounded unto many. And not as it was by *one* that sinned, so is the gift: for the judgment was by *one* to condemnation, but the free gift is of many offences unto justification," or righteousness. So the contrast is between condemnation and justification, or righteousness. Death came by sin. "For if by *one man's* offense death reigned by *one*; much more they which receive abundance of grace and of the gift of righteousness shall reign in life by *one*, Jesus Christ. Therefore, as by the offense of *one*, judgment came upon all men to condemnation; even so by the righteousness of *one* the free gift came upon all men unto justification of life. For as by *one man's* disobedience many were made [or 'became,' or Dr. Young's translation, 'many were constituted'] sinners; so by the obedience of *one* shall many be made [or constituted] righteous."

Now see the contrast between the first Adam and the second Adam; the first father of the family and the second father of the family. From one, judgment to condemnation; the other, justification of life. Through the disobedience of one, many were constituted sinners; through the obedience of one, many were constituted sinners; through the obedience of one, many were constituted righteous in him.

And the idea further that Jesus Christ gave himself to us. Think of that for a moment. It is not that Jesus Christ, as some one apart from us, as it were entirely outside of our connection in any way, just simply came forward and said, "I will die for man." No, he became man, and divinity was given to the human family in Jesus Christ. But divinity was joined to humanity by birth, and Jesus Christ became flesh and blood relation, — near of kin to every one of us.

Read the foreshadowing of that in Leviticus 55:47-49: "And if a sojourner or stranger wax rich by thee, and thy brother that dwelleth by him wax poor, and sell himself upon the stranger or sojourner by thee, or to the stock of the stranger's family, after that he is sold he may be redeemed again; one of his brethren may redeem him, either his uncle or his uncle's son may redeem him, or any that is nigh of kin unto him of his family may redeem him; or if he be able, he may redeem himself." Now that is where humanity is. Humanity is sold under sin. Now if humanity is able, it may redeem itself. Is it able? Is humanity able to redeem itself? No. Well, then, some one that is nigh of kin may redeem it. But who is nigh of kin that is able to redeem it? He who took part of our same flesh and blood. So that, as is expressed in Ephesians 5:30, "We are members of his body and of his flesh, and of his bones." And he is nigh of kin.

Now read again in Hebrews 2:11, and see how this relation is recognized. "For both he that sanctifieth and they who are sanctified are all of one: for which cause he is not ashamed to call them brethren, saying, I will declare thy name unto my brethren." You remember in his last prayer, just at the close of his work (John 17:26), he says, "And I have declared unto them thy name." "I will declare thy name unto my brethren." And he did it; and one of his last words was, "I have declared unto them thy name." They were his brethren. "I will declare thy name unto my brethren, in the midst of the church will I sing praise unto thee." And again, "I will put my trust in him." And again, "Behold, I and the children which God hath given me." Second father of the family. Behold the children.

Mark 3:31: "There came then his brethren and his mother [Now these were those that were actually related to him by the ties of the natural flesh], and standing without, sent unto him, calling him. And the multitude sat about him, and they said unto him, Behold thy mother and thy brethren without seek for thee. And he answered them, saying, Who is my mother, or my brethren? And he looked round about on them that sat about him, and said, Behold my mother and my brethren! For whosoever shall do the will of God, the same is my brother, and my sister, and mother." That is, whoever is born into this family of God is as closely related to Jesus Christ, and that by flesh and blood, as is a mother to her own son.

Read in Luke 11:27, 28, and it is a touching thought: "And it came to pass as he spake these things, a certain woman of the company lifted up her voice, and said unto him, Blessed is the womb that bare thee, and the paps which thou hast sucked." As this woman looked upon Jesus Christ and heard his teachings, there arose in that mother's heart a feeling of what a wonderfully blessed thing it must be to be so closely united to that man as is a mother to her child. What did he reply? Oh, he said, "Yea, rather, blessed are they that hear the word of God, and keep it." Because they are united every one of them to him just as is a mother to her own child. That is, by the very closest ties possible in this world is every son of God united to Jesus Christ, his Brother, his Father, his Saviour, his Redeemer.

SERMON 2

ALL IN HIM

IDO not ask this evening that you should comprehend the lesson of this hour, but I do ask that whatever the Word says may be received and believed; because it is only in that way that we can do anything with the lesson of this hour. The Jews lost one of the very best lessons, in fact the lesson of all lessons that Christ endeavored to teach them, because "they strove among themselves, saying, How can this man give us his flesh to eat," and the same spirit would shut up our minds and hearts to the lesson of this hour.

Colossians 2:10: "And ye are complete in him." And the special thought of our study at this time will be the further development of that idea expressed in Hebrews 7:9, 10: "And as I may so say, Levi also who received tithes, paid tithes in Abraham, for he was yet in the loins of his father when Melchisedec met him."

Our study Friday evening was to learn concerning the head of this divine-human family. "Levi paid tithes in Abraham, for he was yet in the loins of his father when Melchisedec met him." What did we do in him, the father of this spiritual family, this divine-human family? "And the Word was made flesh and dwelt among us." John 1:14. I wish to read three or four texts to show that according to the general tenor of the subject and at the same time following more strictly the original text, we may read this: "And the Word was made flesh and dwelt *in* us." To express the general idea that God was manifested in the flesh among men, we have the text in Matthew's gospel, first chapter, 23rd verse. "Behold a virgin shall be with child and shall bring forth a son and thou shalt call his name Emmanuel, which being interpreted is, God with us," and this is a different expression, both in the English and in the original, "Emmanuel, God with us." But here are other texts where the rendering follows the same original and translates it *in* us." 1 John 4:13: "Hereby know we that we dwell in him and he in us," not among us, but *"in* us." Third chapter, 24th verse: "And he that keepeth his commandments dwelleth in Him and He in him. And hereby we know that he abideth *in* us," not among us, *"in* us, by the spirit which he hath given us." "That they all may be one; even as thou, Father, art in me, and I in thee, that they also may be *in* us." John 17:21. R.V.

In all these texts you will observe that it would destroy the whole meaning to say "among us," and while it does not destroy the meaning in John 1:14 to say, "He dwelt among us," yet it seems to me to lose sight of the very best of the meaning. "He was made flesh and dwelt *in* us." That is to say that Jesus Christ was the representative of humanity, and all humanity centered in him, and when he took flesh, he took humanity. He took humanity and he became the father of this divine-human family, and he became the father by joining himself in this way to humanity, and the flesh which he took and in which he dwelt was our flesh, and we were there in him, and he in us, just as Levi was there in Abraham; and just as what Abraham did, Levi did in Abraham, so what Jesus Christ in the flesh did, we did in him. And this is the most glorious truth in Christianity. It is Christianity itself, it is the very core and life and heart of Christianity. He took our flesh, and our humanity was found in him, and what he did, humanity did in him.

Now, let us follow the development of that idea further. "Blessed be the God and Father of our Lord Jesus Christ who has blessed us with every spiritual blessing in the heavenly places in Christ." Ephesians 1:3. R.V. That is, when he put all those spiritual blessings upon Christ when he was here in the flesh, he put those blessings upon us, because he was made flesh and dwelt *in us*, and we were there in him, and the time when we were blessed with all spiritual blessings in Christ was when those blessings were put upon Jesus Christ who dwelt in us; and the only question for us is, Have we enjoyed, have we received, the blessings that he gave us in him? Fourth verse: "According as he hath chosen us *in him* before the foundation of the world." When he chose Jesus Christ, he chose us in him, and we were chosen before the foundation of the world in him; not you and I as individuals chosen above other individuals, and our salvation personally assured as distinct from others, but *every one in him* was chosen. *Every one in him* was chosen. Every member of this divine-human family was chosen when he was chosen, because we were there in him, and because he was made flesh and dwelt *in us*.

Sixth verse: "To the praise of the glory of his grace wherein he hath made us accepted in the beloved," and when the Father said to his Son, "This is my beloved Son, in whom I am well pleased," he said the same words to every son in this divine-human family. "Thou art my beloved son in whom I am well pleased" in him, *in him*. Was he accepted? So are we in him. Are we accepted because of any thing that we are, or have been, or can be? No, but we were accepted in him, in the beloved. It is so, in him, accepted.

The 11th verse: "In whom also we have obtained an inheritance" in him. Did he redeem the inheritance? Did he buy back the inheritance? Did he pay the price? Did the thorns rest upon his brow in token of the fact that he bore the curse of the earth, and that he bore suffering for the earth, and that he was removing the curse from the earth, and that he was bringing back the inheritance? We obtained the inheritance *in him*, and so he obtained the inheritance and redeemed the inheritance, and bought back the inheritance. We obtained it, because we were there in him, and because he was made flesh and dwelt in us.

"For we are his workmanship, created in Christ Jesus." When the new man, the divine human man, the man Christ Jesus, was created, we were created in him. All members of this divine human family were created in him, "For we are his workmanship, created in Christ Jesus for good works which God aforetime prepared that we should walk in them." Ephesians 2:10. R.V. When did he prepare the good works in which we are to walk? Why, *in him*. What are *we* to do? To walk in the good works that God hath before prepared, that we should walk in them, so the Scripture says in 1 John 2:6, "He that saith he abideth in him, ought himself also so to walk, even as he walked," not so much as an obligation, but as a consequence. Why? Inasmuch as God prepared aforetime the good works for us to walk in why, "He that saith he abideth in him ought himself so to walk even as he walked," not as an obligation, but as a consequence, he "ought so to walk even as he walked," because he is *in him*.

So we read in Colossians 2:6, "As ye have therefore received Christ Jesus the Lord, so walk ye in him." *In him*. Now we were created in Christ Jesus for good works, and God has prepared those good works aforetime for us to walk in them, and how shall we walk in those good works which he has prepared for us to walk in? Why, walk in him. Let us read Ephesians 2:6, and I will read the translation in the Syriac Version of the clause that I wish especially to emphasize, "And hath raised us up together;" and the fifth verse shows that is together with Christ, because it says, "Hath quickened us together with Christ:" "And hath raised us up together, and seated us with him in heaven in Jesus the messiah." "He *hath seated us in heaven in Jesus* the Messiah." He was made flesh and dwelt in us, and with that same flesh of humanity he went to heaven, and when he had purged our sins, sat down on the right hand of the throne of the Majesty on high. When he went to heaven, we went *in him*. When he was seated on the right hand of the throne of the Majesty on high, we were seated there *in him*. Humanity is in heaven. We, our humanity, our flesh, is there, and we are seated there *in him*, because he is the Father of this family, and because every son is in him just as Levi was in Abraham, and when Abraham paid tithes, Levi paid tithes *in him*, although he was not born yet. And when Jesus Christ went to heaven, every child of his went there *in him*. When he took his seat at the right hand of the throne of the Majesty on high, every child was seated there in him; thank the Lord!

Every one of these truths is worthy of an hour's study. The whole thought is overwhelming; what God has done for us, the human family! What he has done to bring us back to him, to restore his image in us, to redeem us, the condescension of Jesus Christ to come here and dwell in us! to take our flesh, our sinful flesh, to unite himself to the human family, to become the Father of the family, to join himself with us by birth, in those closest ties, never to be broken! That is the love of God in Jesus Christ! And he did not simply come here as an outsider, and do something, but he came here and became what we are; he dwelt in us! He gathered together in himself all humanity, and he invited the Father to treat him as the representative of humanity, and so what he did we did in him, and are receiving the benefits of it. What we have done he did not do; but he was treated as if he had done it, and he received the benefits of that, — completely changing places with us! That was the love of God in Jesus Christ.

We read again in Romans 6:6, Revised Version, "Knowing this, that our old man was crucified with him, that the body of sin might be done away, that we should no longer be in bondage to sin; for he that hath died is justified from sin. But if we died with Christ, we believe that we shall also live with him." Tenth verse: "For the death that he died (and we died with him), he died unto sin once, but the life that he lives, he lives unto God, even so reckon ye also yourselves to be dead indeed unto sin, but alive unto God in Christ Jesus." He died, we died with him.

2 Corinthians 5:14 expresses the same idea, and brings it out clearly in the Revised Version. "For the love of Christ constraineth us, because we thus judged that one died for all, therefore all died." Read it in Hebrews 2:9: "But we see Jesus, who was made a little lower than the angels for the suffering of death, crowned with glory and honor that he by the grace of God should taste death for every man." How could he taste death for every man? Because every man was in him; because he clothed his divinity with humanity; because humanity was all centered in him. Notice how many ways this is touched upon in the Scriptures. "He was tempted in all points like as we are;" the temptations of humanity met in him. "All of us like sheep have wandered, each to his own way we have turned, and Jehovah hath caused to meet on him the punishment of us all." Isaiah 53:6, Dr. Young's Translation: "Everything met in him." "Made him to be sin," not a sinner, but "made him to be sin for us, who knew no sin." He took it all, he bore all our sins. See it in this same 53rd chapter of Isaiah, 4th verse: "Surely he hath borne our griefs and carried our sorrows, yet we did esteem him stricken, smitten of God, and afflicted; but he was wounded for our transgressions, he was bruised for our iniquities. The chastisement of our peace was upon him, and with his stripes we are healed. Why? Because our humanity bore those stripes, and we received those stripes *in him*.

See how this thought is further brought out in Romans 7:4, R.V: "Wherefore, my brethren, ye also were made dead to the law through the body of Christ:" "were *made* dead." Notice the form of the expression, — "were made dead." It refers to a definite point of past time when this thing all took place. Now notice further on that idea. Hebrews 10:5: "Wherefore, when he cometh into the world, he saith, Sacrifice and offering thou wouldst not, but a body hast thou prepared me." Margin, "thou hast fitted to me." Syriac Version, "thou hast clothed me with a body." He was made flesh, and dwelt in us; so we were the body, and he put us on, in order that we might put him on, because the Scripture says, "Put ye on the Lord Jesus Christ." But we never could have put him on, had he not first put us on. But, Hebrews 10:10, R.V.: "By which will we have been sanctified through the offering of the body of Jesus Christ once for all." Now how was it possible that we should be made, or were made, dead to the law through the body of Christ? Because he was clothed with a body, he was made flesh and dwelt in us, and we were there in him, and that body of flesh was a body of sinful flesh (Romans 8:3), so we may be sure it was like ours. So when he was offered, he paid the penalty of the law. But that body was our flesh, and we were there in him. And by the offering of the body of Christ, we became dead to the law through that body, because humanity (humanity in which divinity was enshrined) was paying the price. Divinity and humanity were joined in the body of Christ, and the penalty was paid. "Thou has caused to meet on him the punishment of us all;" and we were all there in him receiving the punishment. So we became dead to the law. We were made dead to the law at a definite point in past time. We were made dead to the law through the body of Christ.

Let us read further in the sixth of Romans, seventh verse, R.V.: "For he that hath died is justified from sin." "The wages of sin is death," and when one has died, he has paid the penalty. So he that hath died is justified from sin, and the whole choice with us lies just here, Shall we prefer to die for ourselves? We were there in him and received the punishment and paid the penalty; shall we avail ourselves of that fact? or do we prefer to pay the debt ourselves and die ourselves apart from him? We can do so, but "he that hath died is justified from sin." The eighth verse: "But if we died with Christ, we believe that we shall also live with him." So if we accept that fact and make it our own, that we died *with him*, that we died *in him*, it is thus that we receive life in him, and through him.

Read this same idea in Galatians 2:20, Revised Version: "I have been crucified with Christ, and it is no longer I that live, but Christ liveth in me, and the life which I now live in the flesh, I live in faith, the faith which is in the Son of God, who loved me and gave himself for me." I read the same idea in Colossians 2:11. Revised Version: "In whom ye were also circumcised with a circumcision not made with hands, in the putting off of the body of the flesh in the circumcision of Christ." "In whom ye also *were* circumcised;" do you not see this idea, that everything that he did, we did *in him*? And do you not see that the only question to be settled is, Are we in him? that is all. Are we in him? If so, just as soon as we come into the family, we avail ourselves of all the rights and privileges of the family. Just as soon as we come into the family, we come into possession of all that the Father of the family did. It is feebly illustrated when children are born into the earthly family. They have certain rights in all that the father has done, represented by his property. The child has certain rights and claims, and the law recognizes them. It is a feeble illustration, and yet it is in the line of thought, because when we are born into the divine-human family, and become really in him, by our own choice, it is not simply true that we have a right to certain things that he has, and has done, but *all* that he has done, and *all* that he has, belong to *each member* of the family. Is it any wonder that the apostle John broke out and said, "Behold, what manner of love the Father hath bestowed upon us, that we should be called the sons of God"? Then as sons and as members of the family, all that he did, ours; all that he has, ours; everything comes to us just as soon as we are born into the family, just as we become sons of God.

The next question that arises is, But what about Christian experience on any such basis as this? It is all in him. If we do, it is in him, if we strive, it is in him. It is all in him, and Christian experience may be summed up in this, — what we did in him, then, without any choice on our part, he is to do now in us by our choice. Then we will have plenty of Christian experience of the right kind. All this that we did in him was without our choice or consent, without asking us if we would like it done, he came and by taking our flesh, and dwelling in us, he did it in us and we did it in him without even asking for it, without any choice, without any effort on our part whatever.

Now his desire is that what was done then in him without any choice or will on our part, he shall now do in us by our choice and by our will, and our choice is all the time to be exercised on this point: Shall I remain in him? Shall I continue to choose him, and be in him? That is Christian experience. That is the experience set forth by the apostle Paul in his letter to the Galatians, first chapter, fifteenth and sixteenth verses: "But when it pleased God who separated me from my mother's womb and called me by His grace, to reveal his Son in me." It is now a good time to say that this union by which we are in him is of that nature that it is impossible except as he also is in us. And so reveal His Son "in me."

See this thought in 1 Timothy 1:16: "Howbeit, for this cause I obtained mercy that in me first Jesus Christ might show forth all long-suffering." Jesus Christ showed forth all long-suffering. It was shown forth when Jesus Christ was here, and he desired that the same thing should be shown forth in the apostle Paul. See this thought in 1 John 4:2, 3 and 4: "Hereby know ye the Spirit of God. Every spirit that confesseth that Jesus is come in the flesh is of God." Now it is not every one who confesseth that Jesus Christ *did* come in the flesh, but every one who confesseth, who is confessing, that Jesus Christ *is* come in his own flesh. But you say, It cannot mean that. We will stop a moment. Every spirit that does that is of God. Now when Jesus Christ was here in the flesh, every time the devils met him, they recognized him as Jesus Christ in the flesh. They said, "We know thee who thou art, the holy one of God." Were they of God? Does it meet this idea to say every one that confesseth that Jesus Christ is come, that he did come? The devils confessed that very thing, and that is the very kind of faith that is being pushed upon the people now. The devils believe and tremble, but they do not believe unto righteousness, and believing unto righteousness is the gospel, — is Christ in you the hope of glory, — and every one that is confessing that Christ is come in the flesh is the one that is confessing that Jesus Christ is in him the hope of glory. That spirit is of God. Every spirit that confesseth not that Jesus Christ is come in the flesh is not of God, and it is that spirit of antichrist, and it does not make any difference where you meet it, nor when you meet it. Every spirit that confesseth not that Jesus Christ is come in the flesh is an opposer; he is antichrist and is of the spirit that opposes, and it is the very essence of antichrist to deny that fact which is the basis, in the first place, the general basis of Christianity, and in the second place is the life and the all and in all of every individual's Christianity, and that is that Christ is come in his own flesh, and that Jesus Christ is in him the hope of glory.

SERMON 3

CHRISTIAN EXPERIENCE

WE will continue at this time the study of Christian experience and how it is obtained. "Him who knew no sin he made to be sin on our behalf, that we might become the righteousness of God in him." 2 Corinthians 5:21. R.V. "But of him are ye in Christ Jesus, who was made unto us wisdom from God, and righteousness, and sanctification, and redemption; that we might become the righteousness of God in him." 1 Corinthians 1:30. R.V. "Therefore by the deeds of the law there shall no flesh be justified in his sight, for by the law is the knowledge of sin. But now the righteousness of God without the law is manifest, being witnessed by the law and the prophets. Even the righteousness of God (and that is what we are made *in him* that we might become the righteousness of God in him), which is by faith in Jesus Christ unto all and upon all them that believe, for there is no difference." Romans 3:20-22. Now the righteousness of God is witnessed by the law and the prophets, and it is acceptable because Jesus Christ is made that to us, that we might become that in him, and the righteousness of God will meet the requirements of Christian experience.

When we become the righteousness of God in Him, that will meet every demand here and hereafter, and that is Christian experience, but it is all *in Him*, always *in Him*. Again let us read: "There is therefore no condemnation to them who are in Christ Jesus who walk not after the flesh, but after the Spirit." Romans 8:1. "There is no condemnation." "There *is* no condemnation to them who are in Christ Jesus." That is all, but that is enough. But was he not condemned? And were we not condemned in him? Let us read the record of Christ's experience when he was before the High Priest: "Ye have heard the blasphemy; what think ye? And they all condemned him to be guilty of death." Mark 14:64. They all condemned him to be guilty of death. "And one of the malefactors which were hanged railed on him, saying, If thou be the Christ, save thyself and us. But the other answering rebuked him, saying, Dost thou not fear God, seeing thou art in the same condemnation? And we indeed justly; for we receive the due reward of our deeds: but this man hath done nothing amiss." Luke 23:39-41. "Pilate said unto him, What is truth? And when he had said this, he went out again unto the Jews and said unto them, I find in him no fault at all." John 18:38. "Behold I bring him forth to you, so that ye may know that I find no fault in him." John 19:4. "Pilate said unto them, Take ye him and crucify him, I find no fault in him." Verse 6. "Ye men of Israel, hear these words, Jesus of Nazareth, a man [observe — a *man*] approved of God among you by miracles and wonders and signs." Acts 2:22. One more scripture: "For not he that commendeth himself is approved, but whom the Lord commendeth." 2 Corinthians 10:18. The record is plain. Jesus Christ was condemned by the religious leaders of his day to be guilty of death, but one of the malefactors who was hanged with him knew that it was an unjust condemnation, and said so. Pilate, who represented the civil power, said three times, "I find no fault in him," and yet under the pressure brought to bear upon him by the religious leaders, he told them, "Take ye him, and crucify him," but the testimony is that He was a man approved of God.

This lesson applies very closely to our own situation, "There is therefore now no condemnation to those who are in Christ Jesus," and yet the very ones who are in Christ Jesus are the ones who will be condemned by the religious leaders of this day, and under the pressure of the religious leaders, the civil power will yield and persecute, but — "a man approved of God." And "there is no condemnation to them that are in Christ Jesus." That is, God does not condemn, and what does it matter if man condemns? That counts nothing. And when the Scripture says that Jesus of Nazareth was a man approved of God, it says that every man who is in him is also approved of God.

One thought further: Notice what the Scripture says, "There is therefore now no *condemnation*." It does not say, "There is therefore now no *conviction*." In earthly courts, the first thing is to secure a conviction, the next thing is to pass sentence. The first office of the Holy Spirit is to convict of sin, but not for the purpose of condemning, but for the purpose of issuing a free pardon. so there may be conviction, but do not mistake conviction for condemnation. The very next office of the Spirit is to convict or convince of righteousness, and God's purpose in bringing conviction is always that he may issue a free pardon, not to condemn.

There is one further thought suggested by this text: "No condemnation to them who are *in Christ Jesus.*" Now call up the 35th chapter of Numbers. We cannot take the time to read the chapter, but we can call up the outline of it. It is the record of the appointment of the cities of refuge, and you remember that when one had slain another, he fled for the city of refuge. And if it was shown upon due investigation that it was not a murder with malice, or was not intentionally done, then so long as the manslayer remained in this city of refuge, he was safe; they could not condemn him. But if he came outside of this city, then he was liable to suffer the penalty. These cities of refuge were so scattered through the country that it was impossible for one to be within the borders of the country and be more than one half day's journey from some city of refuge, and the roads leading to these cities were always kept in good repair, and there were signs put up all along the highway, "REFUGE," so the one who was fleeing might lose no time and make no mistakes on his way. Do you see how perfectly the lesson applies? Jesus Christ is not far from any one of us; the way to him is made just as easy as God can make it, and the way is always open and kept in repair, and he has pointers up in every place pointing to Jesus Christ, the Refuge, and just as soon as one is *in him*, he is safe from the pursuer just as long as he stays *in him*. If he gets outside of him, it is at his own risk. He is likely then to pay the penalty, but if he abides in him, he is safe. "There is no condemnation."

In the epistle to the Philippians, 3:4-9: "What things ere gain to me, those I counted loss for Christ, yea, doubtless, and I count all things but loss for the excellency of the knowledge of Christ Jesus my Lord; for whom I have suffered the loss of all things, and do count them but dung that I may win Christ and be found *in him*, not having mine own righteousness which is of the law, but that which is through the faith of Christ, the righteousness of God which we become *in him*. Paul's experience was that of a perfect Pharisee. He gives the list of good things, his birth, his descent, his works, "touching the righteousness which is in the law, blameless," but when he saw himself as compared with Jesus Christ, and when he saw all the works that he had done as compared with the perfection of the righteousness of Jesus Christ, it was not enough that he should count all that he had done simply as nothing, but he saw that all that he had done was actually loss. It was on the wrong side, it was a negative quantity. It must be repented of, and he must *be found in him;*" and when he was found in Him, that was sufficient. And see the comparison between what he found in himself and what he found in Christ, and see the desirability of being found in Christ rather than being found in himself. "In Him ye are complete."

Let us read that scripture in the second chapter of Colossians, beginning with the sixth verse: "As ye have therefore received Jesus Christ the Lord, so walk ye in him: rooted and built up in him, and stablished in the faith, as ye have been taught, abounding therein with thanksgiving. Beware lest any man spoil you," rob you, make a spoil of you, make you naked, strip you. You see we are to be in Christ Jesus; we are to be clothed with the Lord Jesus Christ. Now you beware lest any man strip off that wedding garment of the righteousness of God which we have in him. "Beware lest any man spoil you through philosophy and vain deceit, after the traditions of men, after the rudiments of the world and not after Christ. For in him dwelleth all the fullness of the Godhead bodily," not in a lump, but "in him dwelleth all the fullness of the Godhead," in a body, corporeally; because a body was prepared for him. "Thou hast clothed me with a body." Now in that body, that is, in the flesh, "dwelleth all the fullness of the God head," and all the fullness of the Godhead was in the body, dwelt there bodily. You see the force of that, — bodily, in the body, not in a lump, but because he was clothed with a body. "And ye are complete in him." Better, as the Revised Version reads, "Ye are made full in him." What are we without him? Nothing, nothing. If we try to be anything, we can simply be the form of something. That is formalism. You remember that the law came by Moses, but grace and truth, — or as the Syriac Version reads, "Grace and the reality came by Jesus Christ."

Now it is true that in the law we have the form of truth, but the reality is in Jesus Christ. Now any man who attempts to make himself better, who attempts to meet the requirements of God's law without Christ, is simply a formalist. He has the form merely. It is nothing but a dead form. It is all right to have the form, but the form must be filled. Now "in him ye are made full." The same form is there, the law is there just the same, but instead of being simply as a dead form, a kind of skeleton of the law, it is something alive, and "we are made full in him."

These thoughts can be carried much further, as you perceive, because this idea runs all through the Scriptures. It is everything *in him*. And these thoughts throw very much light upon the subject of justification and sanctification. They have cleared up in my mind much that was dim, that was indistinct, about this matter of justification and sanctification. Let us read again in the fifth chapter of Romans. It would be well to read considerable of the chapter, but we will turn directly to the 17th, 18, and 19th verses. "For if by one man's offense, death reigned by one; much more they which receive abundance of grace and of the gift of righteousness shall reign in life by one Jesus Christ. Therefore as by the offense of one, judgment came upon all men to condemnation; even so by the righteousness of one, the free gift came upon all men unto justification of life. For as by one man's disobedience many were made sinners," were constituted sinners, "so by the obedience of one shall many be made righteous," or be constituted righteous. Now is it not perfectly clear from the 18th verse that as condemnation came upon *all men*, so justification of life came upon *all men*? Perfectly clear. The thought seems to me to be this, — that in Jesus Christ all men were justified. 8th verse: "But God commendeth his love toward us in that while we were yet sinners Christ died for us." Did he die for all? "That he by the grace of God should taste death *for every man*." Now if all human beings should decide at once to repent and turn to God this very hour, would it be necessary for God to make any change in his plan? Do you not see he has done it all, for all men?

Take the parallel again between the first and the second Adam. By the offense of one, by the disobedience of one, many were constituted sinners, — that is, Adam by disobedience permitted sin to come into the flesh, and every descendant of Adam, as a consequence of that one act, had a tendency to sin, and if he would not struggle against it, he would commit sin himself, but no moral guilt would attach to any descendant of Adam unless he himself yielded to that tendency. But if he does not struggle against it, he will yield and sin will appear in him.

Now by the obedience of one many shall be made righteous; or by one man's obedience the free gift came upon all men to justification of life. That is, by this union of the divine with the human in Christ, and by this meeting of our humanity in Jesus Christ, and from the fact that the punishment met upon him for all men, "he has caused the punishment of all to meet upon him." Because of that, every human being receives a tendency or feels a drawing toward righteousness; and if he does not resist, he will be drawn to righteousness, but he will receive for himself no consideration because of that righteousness or of that drawing to righteousness unless he, himself, yields to that tendency. He will be drawn to Christ, he will be in Christ, and then he will personally receive the benefits of justification of life which cam upon all men, just as in the other case when he yields to the tendency to sin he receives the condemnation personally which came upon all men in Adam.

Now to make clear to the eye this subject, I have put it in this diagram:-

$$\text{JUSTIFIED} \left\{ \begin{array}{l} \textbf{By grace} \ \ (\text{Titus 3:7}) \\ \textbf{By his blood} \ \ (\text{Romans 5:9}) \\ \textbf{By faith} \ \ (\text{Romans 5:1}) \\ \textbf{By works} \ \ (\text{James 2:24}) \end{array} \right. \begin{array}{l} \left. \right\} \text{HIS PART} \\ \left. \right\} \text{OUR PART} \end{array}$$

Justification by grace, Titus 3:7, "Being Justified freely by his grace"; Justified by his blood, Romans 5:9, "Being justified by his blood;" By faith, "Therefore being justified by faith, we have peace with God," Romans 5:1; By works, "Ye see how that a man is justified by works and not by faith only," James 2:24. Now much confusion has been caused from our failure to apprehend clearly these methods of justification. Justification by grace, divine grace, is the source of all justification. Justification by his blood: The blood of Christ — and the blood is the life — was the divine channel through which justification should come to humanity, in uniting himself, his life, with humanity. By faith: That is the method through which the individual apprehends and applies to his own case the justification which comes from grace through the blood of Christ. by works: The outward evidences that the individual has applied by faith the justification which comes from grace through his blood.

Now, justification by grace; that is on God's part. Justification by His blood, that is on God's part and he has done that for every single human being on his part. He has done all for justification to every human being; his grace is free to every human being, and his blood is the channel through which it flows to every human being, and "we thus judge that if one died for all, then all died," so that is of God's grace. But while he has done all this for every human being, yet it avails only for those who personally apprehend it by their own faith, who lay hold of the justification provided. It is freely provided for every one, but by faith in him, the individual lays hold of that justification for himself. Then the provision which has been made freely for all avails for him as an individual and when, by faith, he has made a personal application to his own case of the justification which comes from God through the blood of Christ, then as a consequence, as the inevitable result, Christ's works appear in him. therefore for the person in Jesus Christ, it does not make any difference which method of justification is mentioned. If he is justified by grace, as of course he must be, all these other consequences follow. If he is justified by grace, then he is justified through the blood, by his own individual faith, and the works will appear; and you may touch this at any point. If he is really justified by works of faith, when you say he is justified by works, you imply all the rest before it. This ought to do away with our discussion as to whether we are justified by faith or by works, or whether it is by grace, or how it is. One who is truly justified personally, must be justified by every one of them. And when one who is truly justified, manifests one of the four, the other three are all implied.

Now another thought: This justification, this righteousness, is altogether imputed righteousness. Remember that it was given to humanity; that is, this righteousness was provided when Jesus Christ was given to humanity, and it is not something entirely outside of ourselves which he brings, as though some stranger might bring a book to us and say, "Here, take this. This will be a ticket into heaven." No, we do not go in by ticket. He became humanity and he is "the Lord, our righteousness," and when he did that, he became one with us and we are one with him. And God looks upon us as one with him in righteousness, in all that he is, and that is the way our justification comes. So our justification comes by receiving Him who is "the Lord, our righteousness," as that gift to humanity, by a redemptive union, by a life union. Then it is *into*, and upon; it's all through and through; it is not something put on like a garment, but it is *into*, and upon, and it is the life through and through. But it is all imputed; it is all given, and yet there is one idea in connection with that idea of giving that righteousness. This righteousness which we receive was all actually wrought in him and we were in him when that righteousness was wrought, and so that righteousness is our righteousness in Him, none the less a gift, none the less imputed, and yet there is a difference between that idea and the idea of his giving to us something that never had been thought of or heard of before.

We were in him when he wrought this righteousness, but the righteousness which we wrought in him was wrought without any choice or will on our part, just exactly as the sin that was committed in Adam was committed without any choice or will on our part. Now Christian experience is that we shall by faith lay hold of the righteousness, by being born into the family, and then what we did in him without any choice or will on our part, he will do in us by our constant will and choice. Yet it is all a gift, wholly *in him*, and it all started on his side, without waiting for us to ask, "While we were yet sinners, Christ died for the ungodly." He did it all in this way, but it was a most wonderful way, — *in him*. He did it by uniting himself with humanity, and having humanity do it in him. Then when we are born into the family and are united to him, then all that was done belongs to us. But will this inspire the idea of self-righteousness? Why, not at all; because it is all a gift; the grace is a gift, the blood is a gift, the faith which we exercise is a gift, and the works are wrought by that faith which is itself a gift. It is all of him, and yet God's wonderful plan is that it shall be done in him, and in us by this life union, and when Jesus Christ joined himself to humanity, he joined himself to the humanity that is here to-day just as much as he joined himself to any humanity. That is, he joined himself to the whole line, the whole stock of humanity.

Perhaps this idea will serve to illustrate it: He says, "I am the vine, ye are the branches." Now when he joined himself to this stock of humanity, he joined himself to the whole stock reaching down through the ages; and it does not make any difference where you touch humanity, Jesus Christ joined himself to this line of humanity just as much here as away back there. Generations come and go, but the tide of humanity flows on, the branches appear and are broken off, but the stock grows on, year after year. Now when the branches are joined to the vine this year, it is the same vine that has been bearing fruit all the years, but a different branch, that is all, simply a different branch this year. Now here are the branches, they have appeared on the vine in this generation, the fruit of the vine is now to appear on these branches. Is this the same vine that has been bearing fruit? It is not that Jesus Christ was simply a man and that he was right there and stood alone. He was human; he was *we*; all in him. Wondrous plan! Wondrous plan!

But now this idea of sanctification in connection with justification. At first, the sanctification is nothing when the man is simply born into the family, but he is accounted righteous at once when he is born into the family, then he is in him. All his righteousness is an imputed righteousness. He is accounted righteous, and he is completely so. But none of that righteousness is wrought in him. Now by submission, by yielding himself, still being justified all the time by faith, that life, that righteousness which is life begins to work in him, and it is a life union. It begins to become a part of him. So to speak, the life blood begins to circulate through his system and begins to take the place of the old dead matter and the change begins to go on in the system, and he is now connected with the source of divine life, and that divine life is poured into him and circulates through him, and the result of receiving divine life in that way begins to appear, and when that is all wrought in one and through one, — sanctification. Now he keeps yielding, he is justified all the time but he keeps yielding to that flow of divine life and that keeps working more and more; yielding all the time to the motions of that life rather than to the motions of sin that were in his members. The more he yields to the motions of that life, the more his sanctification is growing all the time. His justification, so to speak, is not decreasing any, and yet the sum of his justification and sanctification all the time is simply completeness.

Now his justification is no less all the time, yet growing in sanctification, and it is God's purpose that all the righteousness which is given to one, the moment he is born into the family of God and believes in Jesus Christ, shall be wrought in him by his actual will and consent all the time. In him was life. There is the secret of it all. *In him* was life. Apart from him there is no life. When we are joined to him by birth into the family, then we receive the life. Then the life blood flows, then righteousness which is life comes to us. But the life of Jesus Christ is not a dormant, inactive thing. It is *life*, and life always manifests itself. We are simply the instruments of righteousness. The righteous life simply uses us as a willing, yielding instrument.

MEMBERSHIP IN THE FAMILY

OUR attention has been called in our studies together to the divine-human family, and some of the benefits of membership in that family. While it might be profitable to carry this phase of the subject much further, yet in view of the shortness of the time that we have to study together, we will turn this evening to another branch of the subject, which will be how we gain membership in this family. In order that we may properly comprehend the subject, it seems necessary to consider for just a moment what would have been our situation, had not Jesus Christ come to this world. By that act of sin through which we were constituted sinners, in which sin was admitted into the flesh, we were utterly and entirely cut off from God and heaven, and had it not been for the condescension of Jesus Christ in coming down from heaven to make a connection once more between this earth and heaven, then the human race would indeed have been as though it had not been, — utterly and entirely cut off from heaven. There would not have been a single bond of union between humanity and heaven, not a single point of contact between them; but Jesus Christ came and by taking our nature, our sinful flesh, he made a connection again between earth and heaven, and he came to this earth to bring heaven to this earth, not to mingle it with earth, but to make a connection again between this earth and heaven, and he was divinity here in the world; yet he was not of the world, he was entirely and wholly of heaven and not of this world at all. And he by coming did not mingle earth and heaven together on this earth; but he came to establish a new kingdom; to establish a kingdom in which those who are members of that kingdom shall be just as thoroughly cut off from the world as the world was cut off from heaven before he came. He came to establish a kingdom in this world wherein those who are members should, of their own choice, connect themselves to this kingdom to their utter separation from the kingdom of this world, so that, while in this world, they should not be of this world any more than when he actually and bodily takes them out of this world. That is, every tie that connects them with the kingdom of this world was to be severed by their own will while they are in this world, so that while they are in this world they will be no more of this world than was Jesus Christ of this world, and then when he comes to call them actually and bodily out of this world there will not be a single tie to be broken that would bind them to this world.

Now when he came to this world, he did not bind himself up with the world by a single tie, and when he went back to the heavenly courts he did not break a single earthly tie, for he had not made any. He did not join himself to this world in any way whatsoever. He had nothing more in common with the things of this world, the kingdom of this world, than before he came, yet he did unite himself to sinful flesh and he came to connect earth with heaven; he came to open and to establish his kingdom upon earth, one entirely opposite to the kingdom of this world, just as light is contrasted with darkness, just as righteousness is contrasted with unrighteousness, just as Christ is contrasted with Belial, just as Spirit is contrasted with flesh, just as the world is contrasted with heaven. In all these comparisons it is to show that they are utterly and entirely opposite, and so, "What communion hath light with darkness? what fellowship hath righteousness with unrighteousness?" What is there in common between Christ and his kingdom and Belial and his kingdom?

Now Jesus Christ came and opened up the way into the heavenly kingdom for humanity by coming down into the very place where humanity was, by bringing himself under the very circumstances under which humanity was, by taking upon himself the very load that rested upon humanity, and then by going back. And he established the new and the living way, and he, himself, is the way.

And inasmuch as these two kingdoms are so exactly opposite, having nothing whatever in common the one with the other, it is necessary that there should be a complete change when one goes from one kingdom to the other, and as is always the case when one thing goes from one kingdom to another, it must be by the power of God, and the change is from one kingdom up into a higher kingdom, and that always by the power of God. The tree reaches down into a lower kingdom and takes up out of that lower kingdom that which it transforms into its own life. So we must be born again, or born from above. There was no possibility that we who are in this lower kingdom should in any way transform ourselves, or lift ourselves up into a higher kingdom. So that which made the connection, which is always a life connection, must be life from above, because it is through the power of life that the tree transforms that which is in the lower kingdom and brings it up into a higher kingdom. So there must be a life come down from above into this lower kingdom and it by its power must transform. "Except ye be born again (or born from above) ye cannot see the kingdom of God." So the new birth is the condition of membership in this divine-human family.

Now let us be definite, and inquire what the new birth really means, and how it is accomplished. It seems to me that some light may be thrown upon this by going back to the beginning of this trouble. Man was created in the image of God, and being so created, he possessed a well balanced mind, and was in perfect harmony with god; but Satan came in with his temptation and sin entered, and that well-balanced mind was thrown out of balance and every person who commits sin has an unbalanced mind. And I suppose on that basis, we may say that we are all more or less insane, and it is simply a question of degree.

But the special point is this, that a mind that consents to sin becomes unbalanced, it cannot remain well-balanced, else it would remain in harmony with God. It would run just as he intended it to run, — perfectly in harmony with him, — and when it gets out of that harmony, it is out of balance, and the difficulty began in the mind, and was caused through the mind. The translation which Dr. Young gives of Genesis 3:13 suggests this idea very clearly. When the woman was asked about her eating the fruit, she said: "The serpent hath caused me to forget" and I did eat.

Now that one act of the mind when it consented to sin by forgetting the commands of God, not simply admitted that sin, but threw that mind and all minds that have descended from that mind, out of balance, and the mind, of itself, is no more able to put itself back into balance than a wheel that is out of balance is able to put itself back into balance. There must be a power outside of itself to put it back into balance, and it is the same way with the mind; when once thrown out of balance by sin, it is utterly unable to put itself back into balance. But that mind must be balanced, that injury that was done must be remedied. The way back to perfection is by the same road by which we lost perfection, and we lost it through the mind, and the way back is through the mind, by the power of God in Christ.

Now let us read a scripture that expresses this clearly: "This I say therefore, and testify in the Lord, that ye no longer walk as the Gentiles walk, in the vanity of their mind" [Ephesians 4:17, R.V.].

Now how did we learn that Christians are to walk? "As ye have therefore received Christ Jesus the Lord, so walk ye in him" [Colossians 2:6]. But the Gentiles walk, in the vanity of their mind; Christians are to walk in him, in Christ Jesus.

"As the Gentiles also walk, in the vanity of their mind, being darkened in their understanding, alienated from the life of God because of the ignorance that is in them, because of the hardness of their hearts: Who being past feeling gave themselves up to lasciviousness to work all uncleanness with greediness, But ye did not so learn Christ; If so be that ye heard him and were taught in him, even as truth is in Jesus: That ye put away as concerning your former manner of life, the old man, which maketh corrupt after the lusts of deceit; And that ye be renewed in the spirit of your mind; And put on the new man, which after God hath been created in righteousness and holiness of truth" [Ephesians 4:17-24, R.V.].

It reads it out so plainly that it hardly seems that any particular comment is necessary. That it is through the darkening of the mind and through ignorance that they became alienated from the life of God. Now he says, If you have learned this truth as truth is in Jesus, you are to put off the old man which is corrupt, and you are to be renewed in the spirit of the mind, and put on the new man which after God hath been created in righteousness and holiness of truth. And is it not perfectly clear from the Scriptures that it is by a change of the mind that we put on the new man? And we are instructed to "put on the Lord Jesus Christ, and make no provision for the flesh to fulfill the lusts thereof;" and the new man we have learned to be humanity with divinity controlling. And all new men now created *in him*, when Jesus Christ, the second head of the family, was created, not in the sense that he was a created being, but in the sense that this new arrangement was consummated, that union of divinity with humanity; when that was done, all new men in Christ Jesus were created in him, just as all were created in Adam.

Now we are to be renewed in the spirit of the mind. Read this in Romans 12:2: "And be not conformed to this world: but be ye transformed by the renewing of your mind." This is the way the change is made from this world to the heavenly kingdom. "Be not conformed to this world, but be ye transformed." How? By making new your mind; by renewing the mind. But what is the agency that renews the mind? And what mind is it that is thus obtained? "For they that are after the flesh do mind the things of the flesh, but they that are after the Spirit the things of the Spirit. For the mind of the flesh is death, but the mind of the Spirit is life and peace." Romans 8:5, 6. R.V.

Now there is not the least thing in common between life and death. They are just as opposite, and just as extreme the one from the other as two things can possibly be. They are no more opposite, and just as extreme the one from the other as two things can possibly be. They are no more opposite, no more extreme in their separation the one from the other, than the flesh and the Spirit, because the mind of the flesh is death, and the mind of the Spirit is life, "because the mind of the flesh is enmity against God, for it is not subject to the law of God, neither indeed can be." You cannot take this mind of flesh and put something into it that will change it and make it what it ought to be, because it is not subject to the law of God and the things of God, and the kingdom of God, and it cannot be.

Read on in the eighth of Romans, "And they that are in the flesh cannot please God." It does not say they *do not*, but they *cannot* please God. But ye are not in the flesh, but in the Spirit, if so be that the Spirit of God dwelleth in you, and if any man hath not the Spirit of Christ, he is none of his; and if Christ is in you, the body is dead because of sin; but the Spirit is life because of righteousness. But if the Spirit of him that raised up Jesus from the dead dwell in you, he that raised up Christ from the dead shall also quicken your mortal bodies by his Spirit that dwelleth in you." Read with this 1 John 3:14: "We know that we have passed from death unto life, because we love the brethren." Now in the place of death and life, put these terms in the 8th of Romans. We know that we have passed from a carnal mind, from the mind of the flesh, into the mind of the Spirit, because we love the brethren, and the contrast between the two is all the time that sharp and striking contrast as between light and darkness. Just as marked a contrast as between Christ and the devil, utterly and entirely at variance the one with the other, nothing in common. That is the difference between the mind of the flesh and the mind of the Spirit.

Now every one who is born into this family, who gains membership into this divine-human family, must have a new mind. That is the condition of membership, that is the means of membership, and it means exactly that to be renewed in the spirit of the mind, a new mind entirely. Nicodemus did not understand that. How is this to be? Let us read the answer:-

"Jesus answered, Verily, I say unto thee, Except a man be born of water and of the Spirit, he cannot enter into the kingdom of God. That which is born of the flesh is flesh; and that which is born of the Spirit, is Spirit. Marvel not that I said unto thee, Ye must be born again. The wind bloweth where it listeth, and thou hearest the sound thereof, but canst not tell whence it cometh, or whither it goeth: So is every one that is born of the Spirit." John 3:5-8.

Only those who are twice-born are members of this divine-human family, and the second birth is just as real, just as literal a thing, and is just as essential in order to be members of this divine-human family as is the first birth. It is just as absolutely necessary that we should be born of the Spirit as that we should be born of the flesh in order that we may be members of this family; and the agency by which we are born the second time into this family, is the same agency by which divinity and humanity were united in the second head of the family; because "the Holy Ghost shall come upon thee, and the power of the Highest shall overshadow thee: Therefore also that holy thing which shall be born of thee shall be called the Son of God." Now just as in the birth of Jesus Christ, the Holy Spirit was the agency by which divinity and humanity were united, so also with this, through the agency of the Holy spirit, divinity must be united with humanity in us, and Jesus Christ must come in our flesh by the agency of the Spirit just as he came in the flesh then, and this is all to be accomplished by the renewing of the mind; because the mind is that which controls the being, and if we yield our minds to God, and he can work freely and by our consent through the mind, he will control all the actions; all will be subject to him.

In 2 Corinthians 10:5, this thought is still further suggested: "Casting down imaginations, and every high thing that exalteth itself against the knowledge of God, and bringing into captivity every thought to the obedience of Christ." Now that can only be done, and is only possible when the Spirit of God controls the mind, and when the Spirit of God controls the mind in that way so that every thought is brought into captivity to the obedience of Christ, all the outward acts which are but the expression of the thoughts, will be in harmony with God.

Read further in John 1:11: "He came unto his own, and his own received him not. But as many as received him, to them gave he power to become sons of God, even to them that believe on his name; which are born not of blood, not of the will of the flesh, nor of the will of man, but of God."

They were born of God. How? By receiving him; and what is it to receive him? By believing on his name. Take the same thought in 1 John 5:1, first clause, "Whosoever believeth that Jesus is the Christ is born of God." That is the new birth. "Whosoever believeth that Jesus is the Christ is born of God." Now the whole tenor of the Scriptures shows that that means more than to consent to the fact that that person who came then was the Messiah, because the devils did that, and they said, "We know thee, who thou art, the Holy One of God." But, "Whosoever believeth that Jesus is the Christ is born of God." To show the force of that, read in Matt.16, beginning with the 13th verse:-

"When Jesus came into the coast of Caesarea Philippi, he asked his disciples, saying, Who do men say that I, the Son of man, am? And they said: Some say that thou art John the Baptist: some, Elias; and others, Jeremiah, or one of the prophets. He saith unto them, but whom say ye that I am? And Simon Peter answered and said, Thou art the Christ, the Son of the living God."

And "Whosoever believeth that Jesus is the Christ is born of God." Peter said, "Thou art the Christ, the Son of the living God. And Jesus answered and said unto him, Blessed art thou, Simon Barjona: for flesh and blood hath not revealed it unto thee, but my Father which is in heaven. And I say also unto thee, that thou art Peter, and upon this rock will I build my church; and the gates of hell shall not prevail against it." Upon this foundation principle, that I, Jesus of Nazareth, am the Son of the living God, and that in me is united this principle that divinity dwells in humanity, upon that eternal and everlasting principle, I will establish my church, and the gates of hell, or the gates of death, shall not prevail against it, and they did not prevail against it; they did not prevail against it in him; they will not prevail against it in his followers, because he could not be holden of death. The sting of death is sin, and there being no sin in him, although he was treated like a sinner, yet there being no sin in him, the grave could not prevail against him, and he came forth from the grave, and it is worthy of note further in this connection, that he says, "I will give thee the keys of the kingdom of heaven."

By sin, the kingdom of heaven was utterly and entirely shut against man, and mankind was shut away from God entirely, and he was as it were cast out of heaven and the door shut and he locked out, and the devil's plan was that, knowing that death would come as the result of sin, he should be shut up and locked up in death. But Jesus Christ came down from heaven, and coming down to take humanity, he brought with him the keys of the kingdom of heaven, and he delivered those keys into the hands of humanity once more; he opened the way again into the kingdom of heaven for humanity. He went right into the very prison-house of death, right into the devil's stronghold, and when he came out, he took the keys with him, and as the scripture says in Revelation the first chapter, "I am he that liveth, and was dead; and, behold, I am alive for evermore, and have the keys of hell and of death." And he went back to heaven and he took those keys back with him, but he left the keys of the kingdom of heaven here upon earth, and so he came down to exchange keys, and to put into the hands of humanity once more the power to be sons of God; and when he came, he took out of the hands of the devil the power to shut humanity away from the kingdom of heaven. That is what Jesus Christ has done in coming to this world.

Now the membership in this divine-human family is by birth just as literally as the membership in a purely human family is by birth. It is spiritual while that was natural; this is spiritual while that was of the flesh; and this is of the mind while that was of the body, but none the less real, none the less literal. And it is accomplished by giving up our minds wholly to God. It is accomplished by believing in his name; but this believing included more than an assent to something as being true; believing on Jesus as the Messiah and faith in him and believing in his name means that submission of the will to him, that yielding of the heart to him, that placing of affection upon him, without which there can be no real faith. It is not simply an intellectual act; it includes the whole being. It is forsaking all, then it is receiving all. But it is impossible to forsake part and receive part. This transformation is complete, and this question of turning to God is not something to be done in a half hearted way; the distinction is just as clean-cut and just as sharply defined as it can be, — utterly and entirely distinct, — and I say there is no more bond of union, no more connection between the kingdom of this world and the kingdom of heaven than there would have been between this world and heaven, had the plan of salvation never been devised.

Now sin is just as wholly and entirely separate from God as ever, and he who holds to sin or to the things of the kingdom of this world, in any degree shuts himself off just as irrevocably from the kingdom of heaven as though he never had thought of the kingdom of heaven.

These two things cannot mingle in the least. They are just as distinct as the human and the divine can be. And so this new birth means something. This becoming a member of the divine-human family means something. it means to give up every kind of connection or thought of a connection with the other family. It means the willingness to abandon everything that is of the flesh and connected with the flesh, and turn to God for all that he is to us in Jesus Christ.

Now these things are contrary the one to the other. "For the flesh lusteth against the Spirit, and the Spirit against the flesh: and these are contrary the one to the other: that ye may not do the things that ye would." Galatians 5:17 R.V.

Now I read one more thought in Romans 7:18: "For I know that in me (that is, in my flesh) dwelleth no good thing." In my flesh dwelleth no good thing; *not a single good thing*; not a sign of a good thing in my flesh. "For to will is present with me; but how to perform that which is good I find not." Now that is just where the religion of Jesus Christ comes in, and with the religion of Jesus Christ, the difference is just this: what we will now we are able to perform in him.

MEMBERSHIP MEANS SEPARATION

THE family record of this divine-human family is kept in heaven in the book of life of the Lamb slain from the foundation of the world. And it is a sad thing to think that when the time of examination comes, many now found in records on earth will not be found in the family record in heaven. And there is no question which any human being can ask himself which equals in importance to him, the question as to whether he has really been born again and whether he is indeed, in accordance with God's view of the matter, a member of this divine-human family. So we shall continue this evening the consideration of this question.

In our last study we presented some passages of scripture bearing upon the question of membership in the family, and how this membership is obtained; and we found how complete is the change, by this process spoken of as the new birth, — a complete change from the kingdom of this world to the kingdom of heaven. And we found that this change can only be wrought by the power of the Spirit of God. And that this power was exercised in and through the mind; that it was by renewing the mind; that the mind of the flesh is death; that the mind of the Spirit was life and peace, and that the putting on of the new man was by the renewing of the mind. Having considered these scriptures, I desire this evening to read a little from the comments by the Spirit of Prophecy upon these scriptures, beginning first with "Steps to Christ," page 8 [SC 18.1]:-

"It is impossible for us, of ourselves, to escape from the pit of sin in which we are sunken. Our hearts are evil, and we cannot change them. 'Who can bring a clean thing out of an unclean? — Not one.' 'The carnal mind is enmity against God; for it is not subject to the law of God, neither indeed can be.' Education, culture, the exercise of the will, human effort, all have their proper sphere, but here they are powerless. They may produce an outward correctness of behavior, but they cannot change the heart; they cannot purify the springs of life. There must be a power working from within, a new life from above, before men can be changed from sin to holiness. That power is Christ. His grace alone can quicken the lifeless faculties of the soul, and attract it to God, to holiness."

This has suggested to my mind the idea that by sin certain faculties of the mind were killed, and they became lifeless faculties of the soul. When man was created, the Lord breathed into his nostrils the breath of life, and man became a living soul. Now the outward organization was there before, but all the faculties were simply dead; it was simply outward organization, and the breath of life was necessary, for it to become a living soul. Christ, as it is said in the record, "breathed on them and said, Receive ye the Holy Ghost," and the Holy Spirit being breathed upon the lifeless faculties of the soul, gives life; and that is the light from above. So His grace alone can quicken the lifeless faculties of the soul, and attract it to God, to holiness.

The Saviour said, "Except a man be born from above," unless he shall receive a new heart, new desires, purposes, and motives, leading to a new life, "he cannot see the kingdom of God." The idea that it is necessary only to develop the good that exists in man by nature, is a fatal deception. "The natural man receiveth not the things of the Spirit of God: for they are foolishness unto him: neither can he know them, because they are spiritually discerned." "Marvel not that I said unto thee, Ye must be born again." Of Christ it is written, "In him was life, and the life was the light of men," the only "name under heaven, given among men, whereby we must be saved."

On page 54 [SC 51.4], in speaking of accepting the word of God just as it reads, simply believing God, it says:-

"Through this simple act of believing God, the Holy Spirit has begotten a new life in your heart. You are as a child born into the family of God, and he loves you as he loves his Son."

That is the new birth; on our part, exercise the faith which God gives, on his part, the Holy Spirit begets a new life in the soul. I will read further from "Great Controversy," Vol. 2, beginning on page 127 [2SP 127.3; emphasis supplied]. It is the account of the interview with Nicodemus.

"Jesus with solemn emphasis repeated, 'Verily, verily, I say unto thee, except a man be born of the water and of the Spirit, he cannot enter into the kingdom of God.' The words of Jesus could no longer be misunderstood. His listener well knew that he referred to water baptism and the grace of God. The power of the Holy Spirit transforms the entire man. *This change constitutes the new birth.*"

"This new birth looks mysterious to Nicodemus. He asks, 'How can these things be?' Jesus, bidding him marvel not, uses the wind as an illustration of his meaning. It is heard among the branches of the trees, and rustling the leaves and flowers, yet it is invisible to the eye, and from whence it comes and whither it goeth, no man knoweth. So is the experience of every one who is born of the Spirit. The mind is an invisible agent of God to produce tangible results. Its influence is powerful, and governs the actions of men. If purified from all evil, it is the motive power of good. *The regenerating Spirit of God, taking possession of the mind, transforms the life*" [2SP 128.3; emphasis supplied].

That is the new birth. It is not the Holy Spirit from without, directing something within, but it itself, taking possession of the mind, transforms the life. The mind of the Spirit in that way becomes the mind of the individual and yet not without, or contrary to, his consent; his mind is active all the time in choosing that the mind of the Spirit shall rule in him, and it is the description of Christ's experience when it says he "emptied himself." That is, his own mind, as of himself, was entirely in the back ground, and entirely subordinate; and the mind of God had complete and free sway in him, and self, as of himself, did not appear in Christ at all, and we have never seen anything of Jesus Christ himself as of himself. And yet it was all the time of his own free will, or his own free choice in the matter. His whole work has been to reveal the Father unto man. It may be that in the kingdom, the Father will reveal the Son to us, but the scripture now is, "No man knoweth the Son save the Father." It makes no promise that the Son will be revealed to us here. Going on, it says, "Neither knoweth any man the Father save the Son and he to whomsoever the Son shall reveal him." So it is the work of Christ, with self entirely lost sight of, simply to reveal the Father to the world.

Now the Christian's place, as a follower of Christ, is with self completely and wholly in the back ground, by his own choice, to reveal Jesus Christ who is a revelation of the Father, and so the mind of the Spirit will appear in him continually. The regenerating Spirit of God, taking possession of the mind, and having complete control of the mind, yet all the time by the choice and consent of that mind itself, "transforms the life; wicked thoughts are put away, evil deeds are renounced, love, peace, and humility take the place of anger, envy, and strife. That power which no human eye can see, has created a new being in the image of God." "That which is born of the flesh is flesh, and that which is born of the Spirit is spirit."

The necessity of the new birth was not so strongly impressed upon Nicodemus as the manner of its accomplishment. Jesus reproves him, asking if he, a master and teacher in Israel, an expounder of the prophecies, can be ignorant of these things. Has he read those sacred writings in vain, that he has failed to understand from them that the heart must be cleansed from its natural defilement by the spirit of God before it can be fit for the kingdom of heaven?

The learned Nicodemus had read these pointed prophecies with a clouded mind, but now he began to comprehend their true meaning, and to understand that even a man as just and honorable as himself must experience *a new birth through Jesus Christ, as the only condition upon which he could be saved, and secure an entrance into the kingdom of God.* Jesus spoke positively that unless a man is born again he cannot discern the kingdom which Christ came upon earth to set up.

A kingdom within a kingdom which cannot be perceived except the eyes be enlightened. "Rigid precision in obeying the law would entitle no man to enter the kingdom of heaven. There must be a new birth, a new mind." And that is the climax, that is the point of emphasis in all this lesson; there must be a new birth, a new mind, "through the operation of the Spirit of God, which purifies the life and ennobles the character. This connection with God fits man for the glorious kingdom of heaven. No human invention can ever find a remedy for the sinning soul. Only by repentance and humiliation, a submission to the divine requirements, can the work of grace be performed. Iniquity is so offensive in the sight of God, whom the sinner has so long insulted and wronged, that a repentance commensurate with the character of the sins committed often produces an agony of spirit hard to bear" [2SP 132.1-132.2].

"Man has separated himself from God by sin. Christ brought his divinity to earth, veiled by humanity, in order to rescue man from his lost condition. Human nature is vile, and man's character must be changed before it can harmonize with the pure and holy in God's immortal kingdom. *This transformation is the new birth*" [2SP 133.1; emphasis supplied].

What the new birth is, and the process by which it is accomplished, are certainly very clear before us now. A complete change, a complete transformation of the whole being by a power from without, and that power, the Spirit of God. Now when such a change as this has been wrought in an individual, it follows of necessity that the outward expression of the man will be entirely different. What we say, what we do, the spirit with which we treat each other and others, our whole attitude toward the things of the world or the things of the kingdom are simply the outward expression of the man, what he is within. What he *does* is simply the outward expression of what he *is*. When his whole nature has been completely transformed and a new being has been begotten within him, a new life has been implanted in his soul, it follows of necessity that there must be a different outward expression, and so his life, his relation to others about him, will of necessity be changed. It is perfectly impossible that this change should be wrought within and there be no outward change, and so while outward deeds cannot change the inward man, yet it is perfectly safe to say that when the outward deeds are the same as before, the inward man has not been changed. So while works have of themselves no merit, no efficacy in bringing us to God, in reconciling us to God or in meeting God's mind concerning us as of themselves, yet they inevitably appear in the life of the individual as the fruits of this change, in consequence of this change.

So, as we said in a former study, "He that saith he abideth in him, ought himself so to walk even as he walked." Not so much as the obligation, but the consequence. Now to illustrate this, I would like to present this evening a brief survey of the early church as set forth by the church historian, Neander. It is not possible to present a complete view of it, of course, but only some special points which indicate how these ideas took hold of the early Christians, and how they looked at this idea of a new birth, and to what extent they regarded the religion of Jesus Christ as different from the world. See Vol. 1 of Neander's *Church History*, Sec. 3 (All of these extracts will be from this Section.) A word first from Cyprian with reference to his own experience and his own feelings of this change:-

"While I was lying in darkness and blind night, tossed about by the waves of the world, ignorant of the way of life, estranged from the truth and from the light, what divine mercy promised for my salvation, seemed to me, in my then state of mind, a hard and impracticable thing; — that a man should *be born again*, and, casting off his former self, while his bodily nature remained the same, become, in soul and disposition, another man. How, said I, can *such a change* be possible; that what is so deep-rooted within should be extirpated at once? Entangled in the many errors of my earlier life, from which I could see no deliverance, I abandoned myself to my besetting sins, and, despairing of amendment, nurtured the evil within me as if it belonged to my nature. But when, after the stains of my former life had been washed away by the water of regeneration, light from on high was shed abroad in the heart now freed from guilt, made clear and pure; when I breathed the spirit of heaven, and was changed by the second birth into a *new* man, all my doubts were at once strangely resolved. That lay open which had been shut to me; that was light where I had seen nothing but darkness; that became easy which was before difficult; practicable, which before seemed impossible; so that I could understand how it was that, being born in the flesh, I lived subject to sin — a worldly life — but the life I had now begun to live was the commencement of a life from God, of a life quickened by the Holy Spirit. From God, from *God*, I repeat, proceeds all we can now do, from him we derive our life and our power."

In this period, as at all times, there would be those who had been for a moment touched by the power of truth, but who, neglecting to follow up the impressions they had received, proved faithless to the truth, instead of consecrating to it their whole life; or who, wishing to serve at one and the same time God and the world, soon became once more completely enslaved to the world. Whoever failed to watch over his own heart — whoever failed of seeking earnestly and constantly, with fear and trembling, under the guidance of the divine Spirit, to distinguish and separate in his inmost being what was of the Spirit from what was of the world, exposed himself to the same causes of dangerous self-deception, and consequently to the same fall, as Christians were liable to in other times.

That which our Lord himself, in his last interview with his disciples, described as the test by which his disciples might always be distinguished — as the mark of their fellowship with him and the Father in heaven, the mark of his glory dwelling in the midst of them, — namely that they love one another, — precisely this constituted the prominent mark, plain and striking to the pagans themselves, of the first Christian fellowship. The names, "brother" and "sister," which the Christians gave to each other, were not names without meaning.

You see if they were all born into the family of God and a member of the divine-human family, there is a meaning to the word "brother" and "sister." I have thought of that in view of this study as I never have before, of what it means really to call one another brother and sister; in this family there is a meaning in it.

Nor did the active brotherly love of each community confine itself to what transpired in its own immediate circle, but extended itself also to the wants of the Christian communities in distant lands. On urgent occasions of this kind, the bishops made arrangements for special collections.

This may remind you of the opportunity now being offered to assist brethren who are in need.

They appointed fasts; so that what was saved, even by the poorest of the flock, from their daily food, might help to supply the common wants. When the communities of the provincial towns were too poor to provide relief in cases of distress, they had recourse to the more wealthy communities of the metropolis. Thus it had happened in Numidia, that certain Christians, men and women, had been carried away captive by neighboring barbarians, and the Numidian churches were unable to contribute the sum of money required for their ransom; they therefore applied to the more wealthy communities of the great capital of North Africa. The Bishop Cyprian of Carthage very shortly raised a contribution of more than four thousand dollars, and transmitted the whole to the Numidian bishops, with a letter full of the spirit of Christian, brotherly affection.

The same spirit of Christianity which inculcated obedience to man for the sake of God, taught also that God should be obeyed rather than man, that every consideration must be sacrificed, property and life despised, in all cases where human authority demanded an obedience contrary to the laws and ordinances of God. Here was displayed in the Christians that true spirit of freedom, against which despotic power would avail nothing. We have already had occasion, in the first section of this history, to observe the effects of the Christian spirit in both these directions. In this sense Justin Marty says, "Tribute and customs we seek uniformly, before all other, to pay over to your appointed officers, as we have been taught to do by our Master. Matthew 22:21. Therefore we pray to God alone; but you we cheerfully serve in all other things, since we acknowledge you as rulers of men. Tertullian boldly asserted that what the State lost in its revenue from the temples, by the spread of Christianity, would be found to be made up by what it gained in the way of tribute and customs, through the honesty of the Christians, when compared to the common frauds resorted to in paying them.

The principles by which men were bound to act, in this case, could be easily laid down in theory, and easily deduced from the holy Scriptures, and from the nature of Christianity. Hence, in theory, all Christians were agreed; but there was some difficulty in applying these principles to particular cases, and in answering the question in every instance, how the line was to be drawn between what belonged to Caesar and what belonged to God — between what might be considered, in reference to religion, matters of indifference, and what not. The pagan religion was, in truth, so closely interwoven with all the arrangements of civil and social life, that it was not always easy to separate and distinguish the barely civil or social from the religious element. Many customs had really sprung from a religious source, whose connection, however, with religion had long been forgotten by the multitude, and remembered only by a few learned anti-quarians, lay too far back to be recalled in the popular consciousness. The question here arose, whether such customs should, like others, be considered as in themselves different; whether men might be allowed in such matters to follow the barely social or civil usages, or whether they should set aside all other considerations on the ground of the connection of such customs with paganism.

Again, Christianity, from its nature, must pronounce sentence of condemnation against all ungodliness, but, at the same time, appropriate to itself all purely human relations and arrangements, consecrating and ennobling, instead of annihilating them. But the question might arise, in particular cases, as to what *was* purely human, and adapted, therefore, to be received into union with Christianity; and what had sprung originally out of the corruption of human nature, and, being in its essence ungodly, must therefore be rejected. Christianity having appeared as the *new leaven* in the *old* world — and being destined to produce a *new creation* in an old one, that had grown out of an entirely different principle of life, the question might the more readily occur, which of the already existing elements needed only to be transformed and ennobled, and which should be purged wholly away.

Hence, notwithstanding that Christians were agreed as to general principles, disputes might arise among them with regard to the application of these principles in particular cases, according as they were led by their different positions and tendencies of mind to take a different view of the circumstances — disputes similar to those which at various periods afterwards were not infrequently arising, relative to the management of missions among foreign tribes of men, to the organization of new churches, and to the disposition of matters not essential. Men were liable to err here on both extremes, — on that of too lax an accommodation to, or on that of too stern a repulsion of, existing usages. The aggressive or the assimilating power of Christianity, which should both be intimately united to secure the healthy development of life, might one or the other be allowed an undue predominance. The few excepted who had already progressed farther in the genuine liberty of the gospel, who to deep Christian earnestness united the prudence and clearness of science, these few excepted, the better class of Christians were generally more inclined to the latter than to the former of these extremes; they chose rather to reject many of those customs, which, as pagans, they had once practiced in the service of sin and falsehood, but which were capable also of another application, than run the risk of adopting with them the corruptions of heathenism; they were glad to let go everything which was associated in their minds with sin or with pagan rites; they chose rather to do too much than to forfeit a tittle of that Christianity which constituted their jewel, the pearl for which they were willing to sell all they had.

As regards the controversy between the two parties described, one class appealed to the rule that men are bound to render unto Caesar the things that are Caesar's, — that in matters pertaining to civil order, they are bound to obey the existing laws, — that they ought not unnecessarily to give offense to the heathen nor afford them any occasion for blaspheming the name of God, — that in order to win all to embrace the gospel, it was necessary to become all things to all men. The other party could not deny that these were Scripture principles; but, said they, while we are to consider all outward, earthly possessions as belonging to the emperor, our hearts and our lives certainly must belong wholly to God. That which is the emperor's ought never to be put in competition with that which is God's. If the injunction that we should give the heathen no occasion to blaspheme the Christian name must be so unconditionally understood, it would be necessary to put off Christianity entirely. Let them continue to blaspheme us, provided only we give them no occasion for so doing by our unchristian conduct, provided they blaspheme in *us* only what belongs to Christianity. We should indeed, in every proper way, become all things to all men; but yet in no such sense as to become worldly to worldly men; for it is also said, "If I yet pleased men, I should not be the servant of Christ." We see plainly that each of these two parties were correct in the principles they would maintain; the only question to be determined was, where these principles found their right application.

Whoever followed a trade or occupation which was contrary to the generally received Christian principles, was not admitted to baptism till he had pledged himself to lay it aside. He must enter on some new occupation to earn the means of subsistence; or, if not in a situation to do this, he was received into the number of the poor maintained by the church. To these occupations were reckoned all that stood in any way connected with idolatry, or which were calculated to promote it; those, for instance, of the artists and handicraftsmen who employed themselves in making or adorning images of the gods. There were, doubtless, many who, wishing to pursue these trades for a subsistence, excused themselves on the ground that they did not worship the idols, that they did not consider them as objects of worship, but simply as objects of art; though, in these times, it assuredly argued a peculiar coldness of religious feeling, to distinguish thus what belonged to art and what belonged to religion. Against such excuses Tertullian exclaimed with pious warmth: "Assuredly you *are* a worshiper of idols, when you help to promote their worship. It is true you bring to them no outward victim, but you sacrifice to them your mind; your sweat is their drink-offering; you kindle for them the light of your skill."

Whoever frequented the gladiatorial shows and combats of wild beasts was, by the general principle of the Church, excluded from its communion.

But it was not the participation in these cruel sports alone, which to the Christians appeared incompatible with the nature of their calling; the same censure extended to all the different public exhibitions of that period; to the pantomimes, the comedies and tragedies, the chariot and foot-races, and the various amusements of the circus and the theater.

Now those were simply the popular amusements of the day. That was all. I suppose they did not have at that time some things that we have now, simply because they had not been thought of, and while it was popular then to amuse themselves with the tragedy and comedy, the Christians could not get the consent of their minds to participate in them. They would have nothing in common with worldly gatherings of that kind.

Such was the prevailing and passionate fondness of the Romans at that time for theatrical entertainments, that many were known to be Christians simply from the fact that they absented themselves wholly from the theater. The spectacles, in the first place, were considered as an appendage of idolatry, by virtue of their origin from pagan rites, and of their connection with several of the pagan festivals.

I am reading the history of the church of long ago, but those who read between the lines can read a later history.

Among the pomps of idolatry and devil worship, which Christians when enrolled at their baptism into the service of God's kingdom, were obliged to renounce (the *sacramentum militiae Christi), these spectacles* were particularly included. In the next place, many things occurred in them which were revolting to the Christian sense of propriety; and where this was not the case, yet the occupying of one's self for hours with mere nonsense, the unholy spirit which ruled in these assemblies, the wild uproar of the congregated multitude, seemed unsuited to the holy seriousness of the Christian, priestly character.

Now the transformation is through the mind, and when the mind is wholly engaged with this sort of thing, how can the still small voice be heard and how can the Spirit of God rule the heart.

"The Christians did, in truth, consider themselves priests." "Ye are a chosen nation, a royal priesthood." The Syriac translation is, "Ye are priests officiating in the kingdom of God."

The Christians did, in truth, consider themselves as priests, consecrated, in their whole life, to God; as temples of the Holy Spirit, everything, therefore, which was alien to this Spirit, for which they should always keep in readiness the dwelling in their hearts, must be avoided. "God has commanded," says Tertullian, "that the Holy Spirit, as a tender and gentle Spirit, should, according to its own excellent nature, be treated with tranquility and gentleness, with quiet and peace; — that it should not be disturbed by passion, fury, anger, and emotions of violent grief. How can such a spirit consist with the spectacles? For no spectacle passes off without violently agitating the passions. When one goes to the play, one thinks of nothing else than to see and to be seen. Can one, while listening to the declamation of an actor, think on the sentence of a prophet, or in the midst of the song of an effeminate stage-player, meditate on a psalm? If every special form of immodesty is abominable to us, how should we allow ourselves to hear what we cannot feel at liberty to speak; when we know that every idle and unprofitable word is condemned by our Lord?"

To Tertullian, who was inclined to look upon all art as a lie, a counterfeiting of the original nature which God created, the whole system of spectacles appeared merely as an art of dissimulation and falsehood. "The Creator of truth," said he, "loves nothing that is false, — all fiction is, to him, falsification. He who condemns everything in the shape of hypocrisy, cannot look with complacency on him who dissimulates voice, sex, age, love, anger, sighs, or tears."

Weak-minded individuals, who allowed themselves to be so far carried away by the power of prevailing custom, which contradicted their Christian feelings, as to visit such scenes, might be wounded by impressions thus received, and permanently robbed of their peace.

Did you ever know of anybody's being robbed of their peace of mind in such a way as that?

On the question whether a Christian could properly hold any civil or military office, especially the latter, opinions were divided.

Did you ever hear of any other time when they were divided?

As the pagan religion of the State was closely interwoven with all political and social arrangements, every such office might easily place one in situations where joining the pagan ceremonies was a thing not to be avoided.

That is, if he obeyed the law, he would have to compromise his religion.

For this, all Christians were agreed, no necessity whatever constituted an excuse. On this point, Tertullian's remark was assuredly spoken from the soul of every believer:- "To be a Christian is not one thing here and another there. There is one gospel and one Jesus, who will deny all them that deny him, and confess all them that confess God. With him the believing citizen is a soldier of the Lord, and the soldier owes the same duties to the faith as the citizen."

But, independent of this, was the question whether such an office, considered in itself, was compatible with the Christian calling; which was answered by one party in the affirmative, by another in the negative.

In general, the Christians became accustomed by their circumstances at that time to consider the State as a hostile power, standing in opposition to the Church; and it was as yet, in the main, quite remote from their ideas to expect that Christianity could and would appropriate to itself, also, the relations of the State. The Christians stood over against the State, as a priestly, spiritual race; and the only way in which it seemed possible that Christianity could exert an influence on civil life, was (which it must be allowed was the purest way), by tending continually to diffuse more of a holy temper among the citizens of the State.

To another proposal made by Celsus to the Christians; namely, that they should undertake the administration of civil affairs in their country, Origen replies: "But we know, that in whatever city we are, we have another country which is founded on the word of God; and we require those who, by their gift of teaching and by their pious life, are competent to the task, to undertake the administration of the offices of the Church."

I do not know that it is necessary to add a word. I have read what seems page after page of dry history, that might better be left on the shelf, but some have read between the lines and so have seen the lessons.

If the spirit of God rule in the mind of a man, and control his mind, he will not be hankering after the things of the world all the time, and he will not be wanting to fill his mind with the things of the world, and it may be that he will be so particular that he will think it will not be best for him to attend the popular lectures and the popular concerts. It may be there will be some things considered first class, highly respectable, that he would not think best for him to mix with. It may be that he would rather be called a straight-laced man than to mix with such things. It may be he will think best to withdraw himself completely from the things of this world, and give himself, his mind, his soul, his body, and separate entirely to the things of the kingdom of God, and if there should be such a one, I say, *Amen*; let us go together.

A FEW FRAGMENTS

THERE are some phases of the Christian life and experience that are hard to put into words, and I fear sometimes that we shall make difficult that which is simple in itself, and may becloud with many words that which would be plainer if we said less about it. I do not want to do that. The purpose of our study is not to enlarge upon and draw out some theory. It is to grow in Christ; it is to get help in the Christian life, and although we may elaborate a very nice theory, if it is left there, the whole thing fails; let us not forget that.

We will read first this evening from Ezekiel 36:25-28: "Then will I sprinkle clean water upon you, and ye shall be clean: from all your filthiness, and from all your idols, will I cleanse you. A new heart also will I give you, and a new spirit will I put within you: and I will take away the stony heart out of your flesh, and I will give you a heart of flesh. And I will put my Spirit within you, and cause you to walk in my statutes, and ye shall keep my judgments and do them. And ye shall dwell in the land that I gave to your fathers; and ye shall be my people, and I will be your God."

The best comment on this scripture is in Hebrews 8:8-10: "Behold, the days come, saith the Lord, when I will make a new covenant with the house of Israel and with the house of Judah: not according to the covenant that I made with their fathers, in the day when I took them by the hand to lead them out of the land of Egypt; because they continued not in my covenant, and I regarded them not, saith the Lord. For this is the covenant that I will make with the house of Israel after those days, saith the Lord; I will put my laws into their mind, and write them in their hearts: and I will be to them a God, and they shall be to me a people."

That is the same result as is spoken of in Ezekiel. "I will be to them a God, and they shall be to me a people." And that is to put the law of God into the mind and write it upon the heart. And we have been studying in this very line, as to the way in which God works with us, and how he reaches us through the mind. Now, "I will put my laws into their mind, and write them in their heart." Two or three scriptures will make the meaning of that perfectly clear.

Read first in Psalm 40:6-8, a prophecy of Christ. "Sacrifice and offering thou didst not desire; mine ears hast thou opened: burnt offering and sin offering hast thou not required. Then said I, Lo, I come: in the volume of the book it is written of me, I delight to do thy will, O my God: yea, thy law is within my heart."

"I delight to do thy will," or "I delight *to fulfill* thy will," as given in one translation. This is in harmony with the thought in Matthew 5:17: "Think not that I am come to destroy the law or the prophets: I am not come to destroy, but *to fulfill*." So the prophecy was, "I delight to fulfill thy law, O my God: yea, thy law is within my heart."

I call attention to an expression in Vol. 4 of "Spiritual Gifts," first part, page 101, in speaking of the ark of God: "The ark was a sacred chest made to be the depository of the ten commandments, *which law was the representation of God himself*" [4aSG 101.1]. Now that "law is within my heart," not the two tables of stone, but the law itself, which was the will of God; which was the mind of God; which was God himself in the heart. So we read in 2 Corinthians 5:19 that "God was in Christ reconciling the world unto himself;" and God was in Christ because the law of God was in the heart of Christ.

The new covenant promises, "I will put my laws into their mind, and write them in their hearts," which would bring God in Christ into the heart of the believer; thus that would be "Christ in you the hope of glory;" that would be putting the mind of God in Christ in the place of our mind; that would be giving a new heart. That would be as is described in 2 Corinthians 3:3.

"Forasmuch as ye are manifestly declared to be the epistle of Christ ministered by us, written not with ink, but with the Spirit of the living

God; not in tables of stone, but in the fleshy tables of the heart." The gospel becomes a personality in those who believe, and they become living epistles known and read of all men. But you observe that the whole operation by which this change is brought about is through the mind and the heart, by putting the law of God through the agency of the Spirit of God into the mind and into the heart; and that gives the new mind and the new heart.

Perhaps some have wondered what was the difference in the Scriptures between the word *mind* and the word *heart*. I do not know that I can lay down any fixed rule with reference to these words in the Scriptures. This is more difficult from the fact that our English translation is not uniform in its rendering; but this thought has been some guide to me in studying, and that is: while "mind" refers to the intellect, the reason, "heart" goes beyond that, and includes the affections and the will. We do not find any statement in the Scriptures that *with the mind* man believeth unto righteousness; but the Scriptures do say that *"with the heart"* man believeth unto righteousness." So whatever may be meant in general use by the word "heart," this is true, that according to the Scripture statement it is that with which we believe unto righteousness; and here comes the difference between a true faith and a mere assent, or between Protestant faith and Catholic faith. Protestant faith, or genuine faith, is more than an assent of the mind that a certain statement is true; it includes that, but it goes beyond that, and the faith of which the Bible speaks includes the submission of the heart, the placing of the affections, the yielding of the will to God. That cannot all be done simply by the intellectual faculties; it must go beyond that and must include the affections and the will; and the placing of the will in our religious experience, in the new birth, and in Christian growth, is a very important one. It may be worth the while to read a few statements bearing upon this. "Steps to Christ," page 48:-

"What you need is to understand the true force of the will. This is the governing power in the nature of man, the power of decision, or of choice. Everything depends on the right action of the will. The power of choice God has given to men; it is theirs to exercise. You cannot change your heart, you cannot of yourself give to God its affections; but you can *choose* to serve him. You can give to him your will. We will then work in you to will and to do according to his good pleasure. Thus your whole nature will be brought under the control of the Spirit of Christ, your affections will be centered upon him, your thoughts will be in harmony with him" [SC 47.1]

Also from "Testimony" No. 33, pages 41-43:- "Pure religion has to do with the will. The will is the governing power in the nature of man, bringing all the other faculties under its sway. The will is not the taste or the inclination, but it is the deciding power, which works in the children of men unto obedience to God, or unto disobedience. ... You will be in constant peril until you understand the true force of the will. You may believe and promise all things, but your promises or your faith are of no value until you put your will on the side of faith and action. If you fight the fight of faith with all your will power, you will conquer. Your feelings, your impressions, your emotions, are not to be trusted, for they are not reliable, especially with your perverted ideas; and the knowledge of your broken promises and your forfeited pledges weakens your confidence in yourself, and the faith of others in you. But you need not despair. You must be determined to believe, although nothing seems true and real to you. I need not tell you it is yourself that has brought you into this unenviable position. You must win back your confidence in God and in your brethren. It is for you to yield up your will to the will of Jesus Christ; and as you do this, God will immediately take possession, and work in you to will and to do of his good pleasure. Your whole nature will then be brought under the control of the Spirit of Christ; and even your thoughts will be subject to him. You cannot control your impulses, your emotions, as you may desire, but you can control the will, and you can make an entire change in your life. By yielding up your will to Christ, your life will be hid with Christ in God, and allied to the power which is above all principalities and powers. You will have strength from God that will hold you fast to his strength; and a new life, even the life of living faith, will be possible to you. But your will must co-operate with God's will, not with the will of associates through whom Satan is constantly working to ensnare and destroy you. [5T 513.1-4].

"You must remember that your will is the spring of all your actions. This will, that forms so important a factor in the character of man, was at the fall given into the control of Satan; and he has even since been working in man to will and to do of his own pleasure, but to the utter ruin and misery of man. But the infinite sacrifice of God in giving Jesus, his beloved Son, to become a sacrifice for sin, enables him to say, without violating one principle of his government, Yield yourselves up to me; give me that will; take it from the control of Satan, and I will take possession of it; then I can work in you to will and to do of my good pleasure. When he gives you the mind of Christ, your will becomes as his will, and your character is transformed to be like Christ's character" [5T 515.1].

God has given us the power to yield the will up to him and then he will work both to will and to do of his good pleasure. That is all made possible from the fact that Jesus Christ was made flesh and dwells in us. Now another line of thought: How do we know that we are "in him"?

"But whoso keepeth his word, in him verily is the love of God perfected: hereby know we that we are in him." 1 John 2:5. "And he that keepeth his commandments dwelleth in him, and he in him. And hereby we know that he abideth in us, by the Spirit which he hath given us." 1 John 3:24. "Hereby know we that we dwell in him, and he in us, because he hath given us of his Spirit." 1 John 3:24. "If any man have not the Spirit of Christ, he is none of his." Romans 8:9. "Whosoever shall confess that Jesus is the Son of God, God dwelleth in him and he in God." 1 John 4:15.

Just a comment upon that last scripture. "No one can truly confess Christ before the world unless the mind and spirit of Christ live in him." How do we know that we are in him? In the above scriptures we are told just exactly how we know that we are in him and he in us.

And this work that is thus begun "in him" is to be carried forward and made perfect in the same way. Let us read a scripture that will teach this lesson: "Ye rulers of the people, and elders, If we this day are examined concerning a good deed done to an impotent man, by what means this man is made whole; Be it known unto you all, and to all the people of Israel, that in the name of Jesus Christ of Nazareth, whom ye crucified, whom God raised from the dead, even in him, doth this man stand here before you whole. Acts 4:9, 10, R.V."

When the miracle was performed, Peter said, "In the name of Jesus Christ of Nazareth, rise up and walk." There is the beginning and the continuance of Christian life. The man arose, he walked, and he was there before the council and he still stood, that is, he still had strength in his feet and ankle bones. But how did he retain that strength? *In him*, "Even in Him, doth this man stand." It is exactly so in our Christian experience. We receive strength at the first "In the name of Jesus Christ of Nazareth." We rise in him, we walk in him, we stand, we continue in our Christian experience, in Him. So, from first to last and all the way through, it is always in him. *Always in Him.* And the Saviour has given us a very striking lesson to illustrate and enforce this idea.

The 15th chapter of John. "I am the true Vine, and my Father is the husbandman. Every branch" Where? *"in me* that beareth not fruit he taketh away, and every branch that beareth fruit, he purgeth it [or cleanseth it] that it may bring forth more fruit. Now ye are clean through the Word which I have spoken unto you. *Abide* in me and I in you; as the branch cannot bear fruit of itself except it *abide* in the vine, no more can ye except ye *abide* in me. I am the vine, ye are the branches; he that *abideth in me* and I in him, the same bringeth forth much fruit, for without me" apart from me, severed from me "ye can do nothing. If a man *abide* not in me, he is cast forth as a branch and is withered and men gather them and cast them into the fire, and they are burned. If ye *abide* in me, and my words *abide* in you, ye shall ask what ye will, and it shall be done unto you."

There are many lessons suggested in this scripture. First the closeness of the union between the branch and the vine. What kind of union must that be in order that fruit shall be brought forth? It must be a life union; it is not sufficient to bring them near together; to have them touch one another. There must be a living connection between them. What furnishes the life for the branch? The vine furnishes the life. If it is not a living connection, the branch withers. It cannot bring forth any fruit. There must be life passing back and forth between the vine and the branch, and in order that it shall be this way, the branch must *abide* in the vine. Does a branch abide in a vine when you have it out to-day, and put it in to-morrow, and out next week, and once a week or once a month it is taken out and set aside, is that branch abiding in the vine? The idea is that it must remain there permanently; that it is a union that cannot be broken off at pleasure and re-united at pleasure with the idea that you can get the same results as though it remained firm in that life connection.

You know you can maintain a semblance of life by putting a branch in water, but suppose you forget to pour water into the glass, it will soon wither away. That is, it will lose the appearance of life. Suppose you fill up the glass periodically with water, will that branch bear fruit? How many church members are simply branches stuck into a glass of water who require a periodical refreshing; who claim to be branches and yet never bring forth fruit! And if there is not a periodical stirring up with a revival service, they will begin to lose the appearance of life, and if neglected too long without such a periodical stirring up, even the appearance is gone. *Abide* in me; that is the only secret of Christian life. *Abide* in Christ. You cannot expect fruit from a professed Christian who does not abide in Christ, remain in Christ, live in Christ, in daily, constant union with Christ: cut off entirely from the world, and wholly given to Christ. That is the only way to have a genuine Christian experience.

Now there is one more thought to which I will direct your attention, and perhaps that will close our consideration of this special line of thought. Will you turn to the book of Ruth? The story in the book of Ruth, simply as a story, is a very beautiful one, but when we understand the purpose of this narrative, it adds a hundred fold to the beauty and value of the book. This whole book is to teach us the lesson of the nearness of Christ to us, and that by blood relation; that is the whole purpose of the teaching of the book of Ruth. Of course time will not permit me to read the whole book of Ruth, and I will only outline some of the thoughts in it, and then call attention to the principal points in the story.

After Naomi had returned to her own land, and her daughter-in-law, Ruth, had returned with her, then Ruth went out into the field of Boaz to glean. When she returned, 19th verse of the 2nd chapter, "And her mother-in-law said unto her, Where hast thou gleaned to-day? and where wroughtest thou? Blessed be he that did take knowledge of thee. And she showed her mother-in-law with whom she had wrought, and said, The man's name with whom I wrought to-day is Boaz. And Naomi said unto her daughter-in-law, Blessed be he of the Lord who hath not left off his kindness to the living and to the dead. And Naomi said unto her [Dr. Young's translation], the man is a relative of ours, he is of our redeemers." (See also the marginal reading.) That is, this man Boaz is one who is so closely related to us by flesh and blood relationship that according to the Levitical law he can step in and redeem our inheritance that went away from us when we went out into the land of the Moabites.

Now pass into the third chapter. When Ruth went to lie down in the threshing floor and Boaz made inquiry (9th verse), he said who art thou, and she answered, "I am Ruth, thine handmaid. Spread therefore thy skirt over thine handmaid for thou art [Dr. Young] a redeemer." Going on with the same chapter, "And he said, Blessed be thou of the Lord, my daughter: for thou hast shown more kindness in the latter end than at the beginning, inasmuch as thou followedst not the young men, whether poor or rich, and now, my daughter, fear not; I will do to thee all that thou requirest: for all the city of my people doth know that thou art a virtuous woman." Now we will read from Dr. Young's translation, and see what it was that she suggested in that statement that "thou art a redeemer," 12th verse: "And now surely, true that I am a redeemer: but also there is a redeemer nearer than I. Lodge to-night, and it hath been in the morning if he doth redeem thee, well; he redeemeth, and if he delight not to redeem thee, then I have redeemed thee, I; Jehovah liveth."

When she said, "Thou art a redeemer," she really asked him in that way to redeem their inheritance that was lost by their going out among the Moabites. Now he said, "I will do what thou requirest. I am a redeemer, but also there is a redeemer nearer than I. Lodge to-night, and it hath been in the morning, if he doth redeem thee, well; he redeemeth, and if he delight not to redeem thee, then I have redeemed thee, I; Jehovah liveth."

Now the next day Boaz went up into the gate where all such business was transacted in the Eastern cities. Fourth chapter, first verse, Dr. Young's translation: "And Boaz hath gone up to the gate and standeth there, and, lo, the redeemer is passing by to whom Boaz hath spoken." Third verse: "And he saith to the redeemer;" sixth verse: "And the redeemer saith;" eighth verse: "And the redeemer saith." It turned out that the one who was nearer of kin than Boaz did not dare to undertake to redeem the inheritance for Ruth and for Naomi, and so he stood aside and then it fell to Boaz. It was his right then, as being the next of kin, as being the redeemer who dared undertake to redeem the lost inheritance. So we read in the fourth chapter, fourteenth verse: "And the women saith unto Naomi, Blessed is Jehovah who hath not let a redeemer cease to thee to-day."

The more you read the book of Ruth on that basis, the more clearly you will see that the whole teaching of the book is to give us in an object lesson this teaching that Jesus Christ, the redeemer of the lost inheritance, was one near of kin, next of kin, one who of right could redeem, and one who was able to redeem. And Blessed be the Lord. He did not let a redeemer cease from us.

Made in the USA
Charleston, SC
27 July 2014